THEN AND THERE SERIES
GENERAL EDITOR
MARJORIE REEVES

Ancient Rome

Second edition

NICHOLAS SHERWIN-WHITE

Illustrated from contemporary sources

LONGMAN

LONGMAN GROUP LIMITED
London
*Associated companies, branches and representatives
throughout the world*

© Longman Group Ltd 1959 and 1978
*All rights reserved. No part of this publication
may be reproduced, stored in a retrieval system,
or transmitted in any form or by any means, electronic,
mechanical, photocopying, recording or otherwise,
without the prior permission of the copyright owner.*

First published 1959
Second edition 1978
ISBN 0 582 21574 9

Printed in Hong Kong
by Dai Nippon Printing Co. (HK) Ltd.

Contents

TO THE READER *page 4*

1 THE STORY OF ROME *page 5*

2 THE FIRST ROMANS *page 8*

3 HOW THE ROMANS GOVERNED THEMSELVES *page 14*

4 THE ROMAN EMPIRE AND THE ROMAN EMPERORS
 page 23

5 DISCOVERING ROMAN TOWNS *pages 36*

6 DAY TO DAY LIFE IN ROMAN TOWNS *page 47*

7 EDUCATION *page 58*

8 WORK IN THE WORLD OF ROME *page 62*

9 PLINY: A ROMAN NOBLEMAN *page 68*

10 PLINY ON HOLIDAY AND ON HIS TRAVELS *page 80*

11 PLINY GOVERNS A PROVINCE *page 87*

HOW DO WE KNOW *page 90*

THINGS TO DO *page 92*

GLOSSARY *page 94*

To the Reader

Before we start I must explain about dates. You cannot understand history very well if you are in a muddle about when things happen. This edition came out in 1978. This means 1,978 years after the birth of Christ, and is sometimes called AD 1978. The letters AD are short for the Latin words ANNO DOMINI that mean 'in the year of our Lord Christ'. Anything that happened before the year AD 1 was 'before Christ', or 'BC', and the year in which it happened is called BC. So to find out how long ago something happened in a year BC you must add the year BC to the year AD in which you are living. For instance, Julius Caesar died in the year BC 44. How long ago is that? Add 1978 and 44. That makes 2022. But we don't count the year in which we are when we reckon how long ago things are. (Last year is one year ago, not two years ago.) So the answer is 2021.

Remember years 'before Christ' are counted backwards. That is the tricky thing. Thirty years before Christ is longer ago than twenty years BC. The years go like this: AD 5, AD 4, AD 3, AD 2, AD 1; BC 1, BC 2, BC 3, BC 4, BC 5, and so on backwards.

Words printed in *italics* are explained in the Glossary on page 94.

4

1 *The Story of Rome*

Late in the year 45 BC the Roman general Julius Caesar
returned to Rome from his last war. For years he had been
fighting to make himself master of the Roman state. Many
Romans did not want to have a master, but Caesar had
100,000 faithful soldiers, and many friends and officers to
help him. Fifteen years earlier, when he was a new and untried
officer, the Roman *Senate*, which was the government of Rome,
had sent him to fight the wild Celts of Gaul. In eight years
of steady fighting he had conquered a huge country for Rome,
and had won the heart of every Roman soldier in his army.
But when he asked the Senate to give him his reward they
ordered him to dismiss his army and to return in disgrace to
Rome, because they were jealous of him. Caesar refused, and
since then he and his soldiers had been fighting the armies of
the Roman Senate. Now at last he was master, and the Senate
was beaten.

With hearts full of fear and hatred the Senate chose their
enemy Caesar to be the ruler and *dictator* of Rome for the rest
of his life. Caesar pardoned all the men who had fought against
him. Now he needed their help as Romans to rule the great
Roman *Empire*. He gave them important jobs, made them rich,
and treated them as friends. Caesar's old enemies now sat side
by side in the Senate House with his friends. But they did not
love him any the better.

Soon some of his friends began to say that it was not enough
for Caesar to be dictator for life. He ought to be made King
of Rome, and his family should be kings after him. This was
terrible news. The Romans were a free people. They had got

5

rid of kings five hundred years ago, and not many wanted to be ruled by kings again. If Caesar became king, the Romans would never be free again. Some of his old enemies, and some of his friends, too, thought that something must be done. They began to plot how to ruin him.

But the mass of the ordinary people loved Caesar, and his great army was faithful to him. It would not be easy to get rid of him. So fifteen Roman noblemen made a secret plot to murder him. Their leaders were Brutus and Cassius, men who had received great honour from Caesar, although they had once been his enemies. They knew that he never had any guards or police round him when he was in Rome. Their plan was to attack him when he was in the Senate House, attending to business, and surrounded by *senators*. Suddenly they heard that Caesar was going abroad again for several years to fight a war far away in the East. They must hurry with their plan, or it would be too late.

Next came the news that Caesar was leaving in five days' time. But first there was to be a meeting of the Roman Senate, where he was to be named 'King of the Lands outside Rome'. For the plotters it was now or never. The fifteen men met secretly to make their final plans. They agreed that next day each man should come to the Senate with a dagger hidden in his clothes. They were to surround Caesar as soon as he came in. That night Caesar dined with his friends. Someone asked jokingly, 'What is the best death?' Caesar answered, 'A quick one.' Little did he think how soon he was to learn if he was right.

Next morning the plotters came early to the Senate House; their daggers were hidden in the folds of their cloaks. While they were waiting, another man came up to one of the plotters called Casca, and said, 'Casca, I have learned everything. I know the whole secret.' Casca was terrified, and expected to be arrested on the spot. But the man was not talking about the plot at all. Soon Caesar was seen approaching. In the doorway another senator drew him aside and whispered excitedly to him. This time the plotters were sure that they had been *betrayed*. But no, Caesar moved forward again, came in and sat down on his seat of state, which gleamed with ivory and gold.

The small band closed around him. One of them pretended to ask for a special favour, and grasped Caesar's cloak. In a moment the rest were upon him, steel flashed, and he fell, with twenty-three gashes in his side. As he fell, he slipped and rolled to the foot of a statue standing in the Senate House. It was the statue of Pompey, his worst enemy in days gone by, who had been murdered in Egypt by a cowardly prince to please Caesar.

Such was the death of Caesar, slain, so Brutus and Cassius said, to save the freedom of Rome. It is the most famous crime in the history of Rome, and it did not succeed, because the Romans lost their freedom just the same, as we shall see. But a great deal had happened in the history of Rome before the terrible quarrel of Caesar and Pompey, and the crime of Brutus and Cassius. To understand all this we must go back 350 years to the early days of Rome.

2 The First Romans

Four hundred years before the birth of Christ the Romans were a very unimportant folk who lived as farmers in the plains and low hills on each side of the River Tiber in Italy. They did not even own the whole Tiber valley, only the 30 or 40 kilometres nearest to the sea. At that time they were not even the biggest or the most *civilised* of the peoples who lived in Italy. The Greeks, who then were the strongest and cleverest nation in the world, would have laughed very loudly if anyone had said to them that one day the Romans would conquer and rule the whole of the *inhabited world*, which was the name they gave to all the parts of the world that they knew.

But the Romans owned the rich soil of the Tiber valley where the corn grew thickest, and the low sunny hills where the best grapes and the fattest *olives* grew. Their neighbours lived in the rougher and poorer country of the high hills and mountains, called the Apennines, and these neighbours were always attacking the Romans and trying to seize their lands. The Romans had to fight for their country in many long wars.

The map opposite shows you where the land of Rome was and where their enemies came from. So the Romans learned to become the best fighting men in Italy. They grew tired of always defending their own country, and began to make war on the lands of their enemies—the Etruscans and Volscians and Samnites. They found that 'attack was the best defence'. They also found out that other peoples of Italy like themselves wanted help against their enemies. The Romans began to make

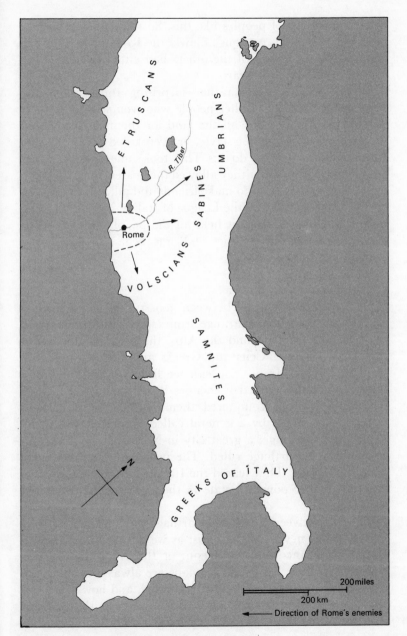

ETRUSCANS

UMBRIANS

R. Tiber

SABINES

Rome

VOLSCIANS

SAMNITES

N

GREEKS OF ITALY

200 miles

200 km

Direction of Rome's enemies

9

friends and *allies* of peoples like this. So they built up a kind of '*League* of Italian Nations'. Slowly the Romans became the chief people of Italy. All the others had either become allies or had been beaten in war.

Other folk noticed a rather surprising thing about the Romans at this time. Other people who won wars over their neighbours usually took all the land for themselves and sold the conquered people for slaves, or even killed them off. The Romans did not usually do this. They took some of the captured land for themselves, but they allowed the beaten enemy to keep the rest. Also they tried to make friends and allies of the beaten enemy for the future. So the League of Italian Nations became bigger and bigger, until it held all the peoples who lived in Italy. Even the old enemies of Rome began to accept the Romans as leaders.

THE BEGINNING OF THE EMPIRE

Next there came a time, between 300 BC and 200 BC, when all Italy was attacked by strange armies who came from beyond the seas and from beyond the Alps, the great mountains in the north of Italy. Celts and Greeks and Carthaginians all tried to conquer Italy. You can see from the map opposite how Italy was surrounded by enemies. But Rome and the League of Italian Nations conquered them all. The most famous invasion was made by a general called Hannibal. His army came from Carthage, a great city in North Africa, and from Spain, which Carthage ruled. The people of Carthage were jealous of Rome. They feared the Italian League, and did not want any other powerful state in their part of the inhabited world.

The war between Rome and Carthage was long and terrible. The Romans never forgot it, just as we do not forget the old wars with France and Napoleon, or the great wars of this century. In their books the Romans are always recalling the bravery of their soldiers against Hannibal, and how cruel and treacherous Hannibal had been. But in the end the Romans 10 won, because the peoples of Italy backed them up. The other

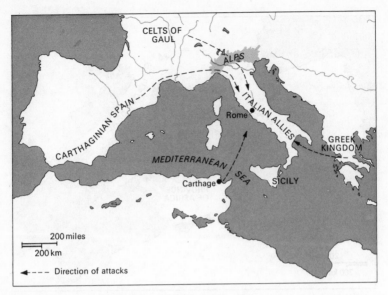

Rome and her enemies across the sea and beyond the Alps

Italians preferred the Romans as rulers to the strangers from Carthage, who would govern them harshly and tax them severely by taking their savings away. The Romans were very strict, but they were fair rulers.

By defeating Carthage, Rome had at this time won all the lands which Carthage once ruled. This meant a part of Spain and a part of North Africa, and the islands of Sicily and Sardinia in the Mediterranean, between Africa and Italy.

Look at the map on page 12 and see how the power of Rome was growing. This was the beginning of the Roman Empire. After this there was no stopping the Roman armies. Italy is a big country, and even then there were several million people living in it.

The Italians were ready to follow where the Romans led them. Soon the Romans were leading big armies against the rich kingdoms at the other end of the Mediterranean Sea. Nobody could stand against them.

Fifty years after the defeat of Hannibal, Rome was the real

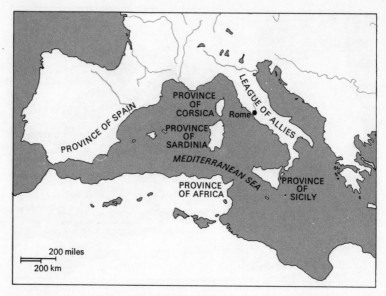

The early empire of Rome after beating Carthage

ruler of the whole inhabited world. All the kings and princes
and peoples of the lands round the shores of the Mediterranean
Sea had either been beaten in war by the Romans or had
become the 'friends and allies' of Rome. But the Romans did not
yet send out governors to govern all these countries. Instead the
old kings and rulers went on governing most of them, but they
received orders and laws from Rome, and sent soldiers to help
the Romans in the next set of wars.

The Romans had won this great empire with the help of
their Italian allies. Two out of every three soldiers in the armies
of Rome were not Romans but Italians. The Romans had all
the wealth and the power and the glory of this empire, but
they did not share it equally with the Italian. These became
angry and jealous. They did most of the fighting: why should
they not share the *profits?* So, about ninety years before the birth
of Christ, many of the Italian peoples rebelled against Rome.
There was a great war in Italy between Italians and Romans.
The Romans won, but they knew that they had been unfair

12

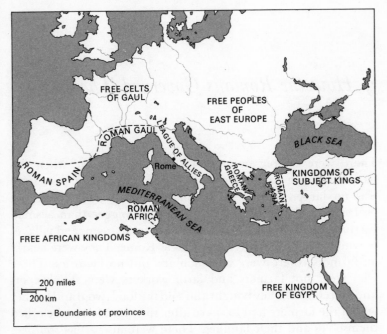

The Roman provinces and the free peoples about 100 BC

to the Italians. So they agreed that for the future all the Italians should become Romans, and have equal shares in the Empire. The League of Allies came to an end. Italy became one state, as it is now, and all the people who lived in Italy were called Romans. All shared in the same rights and the same government.

In the last hundred years before the birth of Christ the Romans discovered that outside the inhabited world there were new enemies. The wild peoples who lived in what is now France and Germany, and in the mountains of Yugoslavia, liked to raid and rob the inhabited world. The Romans had to defend their empire against these Celts and Germans, as they were called. They still thought that attack was the best defence. So it came about that great Roman generals with big armies conquered all Europe up to the wide rivers Rhine and Danube. Later they crossed the Channel and came to Britain.

3 How the Romans Governed Themselves

There were no big nations or states at the time when the Romans began to conquer the rest of Italy. Their own state was no larger than a small English county, like Berkshire or Essex, and the city of Rome was no bigger than a small English county town. There were other small towns and villages in which the Romans lived, as well as Rome. They were nearly all farmers; there were no machines and no factories. Those who were not farmers and farm workers were shopkeepers and merchants. They bought and sold the food, wool and leather which the farmers had to spare after they had fed and clothed themselves and their families. There were also a few *craftsmen* who made by hand the tools and furniture, clothing and weapons of war which people could not make at home. These were very simple and ordinary things. Families made some of these things at home. Not many people bought clothes. The women baked bread, spun wool and wove cloth and made it up into cloaks and *tunics*. But skilled workers were wanted for making tricky things like ploughs, wheels for carts, pots and pans, shields, swords and armour. So there were always a few craftsmen in the towns.

In early Rome there were not many rich people. Most of the farmers were *peasants* who each owned a little land, often no more than 2 to 2·5 hectares. On this small patch of soil they

Opposite above: *This picture shows a coppersmith's workshop. It is a relief, or carving, which was found at Pompeii in Italy, and was probably on the wall of a workshop. Notice the moulds on the wall and the doors of the furnace*

Opposite below: *This is a relief of a cowman looking after his cattle*

had to grow enough food and keep enough sheep to feed and clothe their families. They had to have something to spare also to buy weapons of war. This shows how simple life was, and how hard it was to save much money.

There were some families that owned over a hundred hectares. These were thought to be extremely rich. For a long time anyone who owned as much as two or three hundred hectares was like a millionaire today. The Romans chose men from these rich families to rule the nation and to manage the wars. Because they were rich, such people had servants and slaves to look after their farms. This gave the rich plenty of spare time. The rest of the Romans expected the rich men to use their spare time in the service of their country. They learned to command soldiers and to practise for battles. They had time to live in the city of Rome, helping to rule instead of working in the fields. In modern times most people find it difficult to spare time even to be a member of their local *council*, and to go to the Town or County Hall once a week for meetings. So it is not surprising that in Roman times only the rich families could have a big share in ruling the country.

However, the masses of poor people had some share in their government. Because the Roman state was so small in early times, it was possible to hold public meetings in a great field at Rome. Most of the *citizens*, as they were called, could be present. Meetings of the citizens met every year to choose two governors to rule the country and command the army. These two acted as generals and judges and *presidents* of the great Council of Rome, which was called the Senate. The governors had to do all the work of government, not just some special jobs. They were called *consuls*, and held their power just for one year, until the next year's consuls took their place. In Britain we still choose mayors of a city for a year. All Romans could vote for the consuls at the elections. So even the poorest peasant had a say in choosing his governors. The rich men, or nobles, had to be popular with the poor, if they wanted to become consuls. There were some other governors who helped 16 the consuls, but they were much less important. The Romans even elected the officials who collected the taxes and looked after the money of the Roman state.

The ordinary people also had a say in making and changing the laws. One of the consuls would call a special meeting of the Roman citizens if he wanted to make a new law. He would read out the law to the meeting, and the people would vote for or against the law. The public meeting also decided whether to start wars. The governors could not start a new war unless the people wanted it.

Things were very different from nowadays. There was no *parliament* elected for five years to govern the country as in Britain. Instead the government changed every year. After the harvest, when the peasants had spare time to come to Rome, the Romans chose the consuls for the next year. It was not very easy for the peasants to come in for the other public meetings during the year. So such meetings took place only once a fortnight on market days. Many peasants would come to Rome then to sell their goods, and have a chance of voting. On the market days you could see streams of people walking or riding into Rome from the villages. They would be wondering if any big business was coming up at the public meeting. Someone might say, 'I hear the consuls want to fight the Greeks. I'm all against it. I have had enough fighting. Hannibal was bad enough. I need more time to get my land in order.' Another would reply, 'Yes, but these Greeks are dangerous. Remember how they secretly helped Hannibal and wanted him to win. We had better finish the whole job. Then there will be no more trouble for a long time.'

After harvest, at election time, the citizens would be arguing how to vote. One would say, 'I shall vote for Marcus. He fought very well when he was an officer against Hannibal last year. I was in his regiment. He will make a good general.' But another would reply, 'No. Marcus is from an unknown family. He is an upstart. I shall vote for Scipio. His father and grandfather were splendid generals. He is sure to be all right.'

When the rulers had finished their year of power they did not just become ordinary private persons again. Instead, they 17

became members of the Roman Council of State. This was the Senate, and its members were called senators. All the Romans who had been rulers of any sort, consuls and judges and generals, went to its meetings. They remained senators for the rest of their lives. They had to live in the city of Rome most of the time, and their job was to give advice to the yearly consuls about difficult questions. The consuls would ask the Senate to tell them how big an army to take to a war, or how much money a war would cost, or whether any new laws were wanted.

As the consuls were usually younger than the senators, they would do what the Senate suggested. So the Senate helped to govern Rome. Really the consuls and the Senate could have their own way as long as they did not annoy the mass of ordinary people too much. But as the Roman people could not turn senators out of office by a vote, the Senate did not pay very much attention to the wishes of the people. There were many quarrels between the Senate and the people. The Senate was like a mixture of our *House of Lords* and *House of Commons*. Like the members of Parliament in the House of Commons, the senators could control the actual rulers, and like the members of the House of Lords, it was very hard to get rid of them.

HOW THE ROMAN STATE CHANGED IN LATER TIMES

If there had been no Senate the Roman people would have had a larger share in the government. But as the Roman Empire became bigger and bigger there was more and more public business to be done. The Senate looked after most of this. It became more and more powerful, and paid less and less attention to the wishes of the people. In fact the usual way of talking about the state of Rome was to call it not 'the Roman people' but 'the Senate and the Roman people'. This was shortened in Latin to the famous four letters 'SPQR', which stand for the Latin words 'Senatus Populusque Romanus'.

Opposite: *Elections were held in a forum. These are the remains of the one at Pompeii. You can read more about Pompeii on page 36*

The sort of men who were consuls and senators became richer and richer as time went on, after the wars with Hannibal. Consuls could make great fortunes in the big wars of Rome by robbing the countries which they conquered. The generals came home with cartloads of gold and silver and valuable furniture from the kingdoms of the East. The ordinary soldiers only received a hatful of coins as their share. Riches made the Roman nobles proud. They began to despise the hard-working peasants who voted in the public meetings and fought as soldiers in the wars. The nobles also began to buy up land belonging to the peasants. The poor farmers easily agreed to sell when a rich man offered a sack of silver coins for their farms. But in the end the farmers spent their money and had no land. So they became very discontented with the nobles.

Now it was a custom of the Romans that the common people should have leaders of their own. They elected ten of these each year. They were called *tribunes*, and they had the right to protect the ordinary people from the rulers. If the consuls gave harsh orders to the people the tribunes could order the consuls to stop, and the consuls had to stop doing whatever they were doing. Often the tribunes would stop a consul from calling up too many citizens to be soldiers. Sometimes they would set free a man whom the consuls had arrested and were punishing severely. The tribunes also had the right to make laws in the public meetings, just as consuls did. So in every way the tribunes protected the people.

When the Roman nobles became harsh and cruel, after the wars with Hannibal, the tribunes began to remember their duty. These were many terrible quarrels between the tribunes and the consuls and the Senate. The tribunes wanted to pass laws which would help the ordinary people. They wanted to share out the land of Italy more fairly between the poor and the rich Romans. In modern times, when there is trouble between rich and poor or between workers and employers, there are strikes, and the workers demand more wages and shorter hours. But in ancient times most people made their living out of land and farming. So the Roman poor folk, instead of asking for more wages, asked for more land. The only way to find more land for the poor was by taking it away from the big landowners. Of course the rich did their best to stop the tribunes from passing any laws about land. Really the nobles had no right to interfere with the tribunes. Both sides lost their tempers. There was much fighting with sticks and stones and many riots in the streets of Rome, and in the public meetings of the people. The leaders used to come to the meetings with a mob of followers armed with clubs. Instead of voting, they tried to pass laws, or to stop laws from being passed, by driving the other side out of meetings. The senators were usually better at this game than the tribunes, and in the end several tribunes were murdered.

Now until this time (the year 133 BC) the Romans had been very proud of the fact that the army never interfered in public life and *politics*. As in Britain today, the rulers could only use the police to keep order in public; they could not call in soldiers even to stop a riot in the streets. As the Romans had hardly any police at all it was very difficult to stop all the riots.

Then in the year 88 BC one of the consuls, who had called up a big army for a war outside Italy, persuaded his troops to march against Rome itself. He promised them rich rewards if they would turn against the people. This man's name was Sulla. He backed up the Senate, but some of the senators did not agree with him. They were very shocked that a Roman should lead an army against Rome. They thought that even the rule of the people was better than that. Several of them joined the side of the tribunes. In the end there was a civil war between the army of Sulla and an army raised by the leaders of the people. Citizens fought against citizens. Sulla won, and became master of Rome. He made new laws that gave the Senate more power than ever, and took away most of the rights of the tribunes.

This was not the end of the story. The Roman people wanted to have the tribunes back again, and some senators still supported the side of the people. So the troubles went on at Rome for nearly a century before the birth of Christ. There were also many wars outside Italy during these times, as the Empire kept on growing bigger. The wars needed generals. The best 21 of these generals were Pompey the Great and Julius Caesar. Pompey made great conquests in the East, in Turkey and Syria. Julius Caesar conquered most of France, and was the first Roman to attack Britain. Unfortunately Caesar and Pompey were jealous of each other. There was yet another war between citizens. Caesar pretended to be fighting for the rights of the people and the tribunes. Pompey pretended to be fighting on the Senate's side. But really each was fighting for himself. Caesar won, but he did not even pretend to give the government back to the tribunes and the people. Instead he made himself the ruler of Rome for life, and called himself 'Dictator– for ever'.

That was the end of freedom at Rome. Till then Rome had been a *republic*. There had been no king. Nobody held power unless the people elected him. The laws were passed by the people at their meetings. Even the consuls had not been able to do just what they liked in their year of rule. The Senate and the tribunes had kept an eye on them.

Julius Caesar put an end to all that. He set about ruling Rome by himself. The people did not mind so much, because Caesar looked after them, and said that he was on their side. But he had plenty of enemies. The nobles would not agree that one man should rule. So they made a plot and murdered Julius Caesar. You have read the story of this famous crime at the beginning of this book. This happened on the day which the Romans called the Ides of March, in 44 BC just over two thousand years ago. The story is told by Shakespeare in a very exciting way in his play called 'Julius Caesar'

The murder did not make much difference. The Roman leaders began fighting each other again, but there was no more talk about the rights of the people. In the end a man called Octavian won. He was a nephew of Julius Caesar, and Caesar had adopted him as his son. Octavian beat all his enemies, including the famous Mark Antony, and made himself the first *emperor* of Rome. The Romans were tired of fighting each other and were ready at last to accept the rule of kings.

4 The Roman Empire and the Roman Emperors

An emperor is a person who rules an empire made up of several different countries. The Roman emperors ruled Rome and Italy, and all the lands or *provinces* inside the empire. Octavian called himself by the title of Augustus. He ruled for forty years, and gave peace to the whole inhabited world. No other Roman emperor ever reigned so long or ruled so well. The Romans never forgot him. They called all the later emperors Augustus after him, in addition to their ordinary names, and gave his name to the eighth month of the year, which we still call August.

When Augustus became emperor he needed the help of the old noble families. He wanted the nobles to help him rule the provinces and to run the Roman armies. These were too big for him to manage by himself. The Senate continued to exist, and Augustus used to ask it for advice. But he really decided by himself who should be consuls and generals and senators. All went well while Augustus was alive. The Romans wanted peace at home and victories abroad. Augustus gave them both, and they were glad to have a single man in charge of everything. They could trust him to do his best.

The emperors who ruled after Augustus were not so popular. The nobles were jealous of them and often plotted to murder them. So the emperors became suspicious of the nobles and invented excuses to put them to death. Tiberius, Claudius and Nero are the most famous of these emperors. It was during the reign of Tiberius that Jesus Christ was put to death at Jerusalem, rather against the wishes of the Roman governor, as we shall see on page 28. Julius Caesar had conquered much of south-east England; in AD 43 the Emperor Claudius sent

23

Augustus (left) and Nero (right). These heads appear on Roman coins

an army to attempt to conquer the whole island of Britain quickly, but it took the Romans forty years to reach Scotland. You can read more about this in another Then and There book called 'The Romans in Scotland'.

The Emperor Nero was unpopular everywhere. He was interested in nothing but his hobbies. These were singing and acting, which the Romans thought disgraceful. In Nero's reign a great fire destroyed a large part of the city of Rome. People blamed Nero for the fire, and he became suspicious of everyone. Even the soldiers grew tired of him, though their pay all came from him.

The Senate and the army set about choosing a new emperor to take Nero's place. So far, all the emperors had come from the family of Augustus. Each one seemed worse than the one before. So now they tried to choose a different sort of emperor. Someone invented a slogan: 'The best man ought to be king.' The idea was to choose the best general and governor of that time to be emperor. But it was not so easy to decide who the best man was. Each army wanted to make its own general into an emperor, and sometimes there was a short war between the armies before a new emperor was appointed. But really Augustus and the later emperors ruled the inhabited world very well and very peacefully for about two hundred years. We shall be very lucky in modern times if we have peace for a quarter as long as the Roman Empire had it.

The second century after the birth of Christ was the happiest time. This means the years from AD 100 to about 200. The emperors and the nobles had stopped quarrelling. There was work for everybody. Taxes were low. The armies did not fight each other. Wars were with wild *barbarians* on the frontiers of the empire. The best men really did become emperors. The most famous of these were Trajan, Hadrian and Marcus Aurelius.

Trajan was a good general and a good ruler. During his reign the senator Pliny lived. Later on we shall read some of the letters of Pliny to find out what life was like in those times. Trajan beat the foreign enemies of the empire in several great wars, and added the last province to the empire. It was the land of Dacia, modern Romania, beyond the River Danube. After him there were no more conquests. Hadrian, who came after Trajan, was more peaceful. He is famous for his long journeys

*A Roman statue
of the Emperor Trajan*

round the Roman Empire. He tried to visit every province, to set things right and to see that the army and the defences were in order. He even came to Britain, and ordered a great wall to be built in the north of England. We still call this Hadrian's Wall. It went from Carlisle to the place which we still call Wallsend, and it kept the wild Scots out of the peaceful part of Britain. You can read more about it in another Then and There book called 'Roman Britain'.

Marcus Aurelius was the wisest of the Roman emperors. He had read all the best books of the Greeks, and was what people call a 'philosopher', which means a 'lover of wisdom'. Marcus thought that people should live their lives by certain rules, and he wrote a book about his own thoughts and behaviour. But his wisdom was not much use to him when he was emperor. The foreign enemies from northern Europe had started to attack the Roman Empire again. Marcus had to spend a lot of time fighting them, but the wars were a long way off, beyond the river Danube.

In the two hundred years which came after the age of 'the best men', the Roman Empire went steadily to ruin. Foreign wars became more dangerous. Wild peoples with strange names, Goths and Vandals and Franks, burst into the empire and seized whole provinces. But the real trouble was that the Roman armies spent too much time fighting each other. They ought to have been fighting against the Goths and Vandals. Instead, they were often trying to make their generals into emperors. So the Empire of Rome came to an end about four hundred years after the birth of Christ.

THE PROVINCES

We have talked about the provinces without saying much about what they were. The Romans divided the whole land of the Empire into big areas, each about as large as a small modern country. These were the provinces. Britain was one province. There were four provinces in the country which is now France, two in Spain and one in Portugal. So each province was quite big. It was an important job to be governor of one of them.

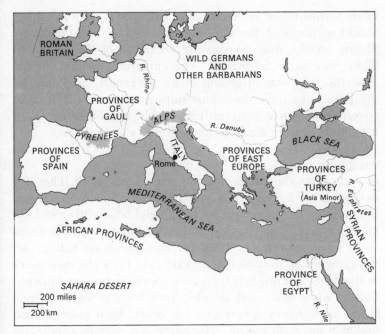

The Roman Empire reaches the great rivers and the deserts beyond the civilised world from 10 BC onwards

The emperors chose the governors, who had usually to be senators. Each governor was helped by a few other officials. These were men who had once been officers in the Roman army.

There is one Roman governor most people have heard of. This is Pontius Pilate. He governed Israel, which the Romans called Judaea. He it was who ordered Jesus Christ to be put to death. Why did he do this? Here is the reason, as you can read in the Gospel of St John.

The Jews told Pilate that Jesus Christ claimed to be 'the king of the Jews'. This would mean that he was a rebel against the emperor. Pilate questioned Jesus. 'Are you a king of the Jews?' 'Why,' replied Jesus, 'who said this to you?' 'Your own people say it, and the High Priest who arrested you,' answered Pilate. 'But are you really a king?' 'It is only you who say this,' said Jesus, 'I have never claimed to be a king in this world.' So 27

Pilate turned to the Jews and said, 'I find no fault in this man. Shall I let him go?' But the Jews answered in the fatal words: 'If you let this man go you are no friend of the emperor.' Pilate was badly frightened. The emperor was the terrible Tiberius, who was suspicious of his governors. So Pilate let the Jews have their way. This story shows how the Roman governors tried to govern justly if possible, but sometimes failed because they were afraid of the power of the emperor.

THE ROMAN ARMY

In early times the soldiers did not get any pay at all. They did not go in for fighting as a job. In those times before Rome became big, her wars were with her neighbours, 30 or 40 kilometres away. These would come *plundering* to steal the crops or to seize some land. Then the consuls would call up all the grown men over eighteen years old. They left their work in the fields and brought their own spears, swords and shields. Battles were short and simple. Two lines of fighting men threw their heavy spears at each other, then charged and fought it out with swords. The battle was over in a day, and wars did not last long. Both sides had to go back home to their work on the farms. They usually fought in summer, after the corn harvest in June and before the grape harvest in October.

The early Roman wars were like this. But as the Roman state became bigger and richer, the Romans began to take taxes from the people they conquered. They used this money to pay soldiers. So the soldiers were able to stay away from their farms and homes for a longer time. The generals had time to train them and to give them practice, like a football team. They learned to charge steadily, and to hurl their spears all together. The spears fell like hail on the enemy. It was no good dodging. So the Roman army became the best in the world. It was also the biggest, because the Romans had all the people of Italy to use as soldiers. They grouped their soldiers in regiments, which they called *legions*. Each legion had about 5,000 men. By the time of the Emperor Augustus the Romans were able to keep twenty-five legions. Can

A relief showing Roman soldiers with long shields

you work out how many men that was? The soldiers now spent all their time in the army. There had never been so big or so strong an army in the world before. That is why the Roman Empire lasted so long.

Roman soldiers wore some armour, and fought with short swords and heavy spears. But they were not dressed like the knights of the Middle Ages, in suits of iron. They wore helmets to cover their heads, but not their faces. They had leather coats strengthened with plates of metal, and each man carried a long shield, with edges turned back, to protect his body. They wore no iron behind them. A Roman soldier did not turn his back to the enemy. If he was hit in the back no one was sorry for him. Usually they marched and fought on foot, so their armour had to be fairly light. You can see in the picture how big the shield was.

After the time of Augustus the conquered people in the provinces, such as the Britons, were allowed to join the Roman army. The pay was quite good. A soldier earned more than a farm labourer. He was paid for every day of the year, and had a lot of extras. The barracks or camps where the troops lived were built of stone, and were much drier and warmer 29 than the huts of the peasants. They were as comfortable as town houses. There was plenty of excitement, even when there was no fighting. Each legion was stationed in one place. So not less than 5,000 men would be in a camp. They could arrange sports and races. They had Roman baths, with warm water. Shopkeepers used to come and make little towns near the camps. The men kept their wives there. When they retired after twenty five years of service, the emperor gave the soldiers either sums of money or else little farms where they could settle down for the rest of their lives. No wonder being a soldier in the Roman army was popular.

If a man was both brave and sensible he could become a company officer, called a *centurion*. Each legion had sixty companies, each of about ninety men. The centurions commanded the companies. They were the most important officers under the commander of the whole legion, who was called a *legate*. The best of the ordinary soldiers became

A relief showing Roman soldiers building a fortification

centurions. They were very well paid, for they earned not less than 4,000 silver pennies a year, over twelve times the pay of an ordinary soldier. So the sons of poor men had a splendid chance of becoming rich in the Roman army. The best of the centurions were promoted to an even higher rank. A poor labourer might enlist as a soldier in the army, and end up as the commander of the Imperial Guard at Rome. His sons then had a chance of becoming senators and governors of provinces. Of course only a few lucky men did so well. You had to be tough and clever for that.

Life was strict in the Roman army. It was famous for discipline, which means obeying orders without asking questions. If you disobeyed or made bad mistakes, you were flogged with rods. If a whole company behaved badly, the officers sometimes put one man out of every ten to death, even if they were not the ones to blame. A certain centurion was called 'old give-me-another', because when he broke a rod on a man's back he used to shout 'give me another one'.

In the army all the orders were in Latin. You would not get on well until you learned Latin. It was hard for the recruits who came from countries which did not speak Latin to understand their orders; but after twenty years in the army they learned to speak Latin like Romans. They made their children learn Latin, and when they retired from the army they helped to spread the new language in their home country. This was one of the ways in which Latin came to be the language of France and Spain in Roman times. That is why French and Spanish as well as Italian people today speak a language that is very like Latin.

WHAT THE PEOPLE IN THE PROVINCES THOUGHT OF ROME

There had been many empires before the Romans. But none were half so big or contained so many different peoples. All these peoples had different customs and spoke different languages. Most earlier conquerors, like the Persians or the Carthaginians, had taken money and goods as taxes from their subjects, and used the people as labourers or even as slaves. 31

They made them build huge *temples* and palaces for the rulers, and they made them fight as soldiers too. But the Romans were different from all the earlier conquerors. They were the first conquerors in history who treated the conquered people like themselves, and shared the good things of their empire with their *subjects*. Even the Greeks, who were very civilised, thought that unless they ruled their subjects very strictly the subjects would rise and destroy them. So the Greeks were always afraid of their subjects, and never treated them as equals.

The Romans changed all this. They had such a strong army, and were so used to winning wars, that they were not afraid of the people they conquered. They knew that the Roman army could always stop any rebels. Think of Julius Caesar, the man who conquered France (or Gaul) for Rome; this was all the land from the Pyrenees mountains of Spain to the river Rhine in Germany. He conquered this with an army of 50,000 men in ten legions. The Gauls could raise over 200,000 fighting men, but they could not beat Caesar. 'Roman Gaul', another book in this series, tells you more about how the Romans conquered Gaul. No wonder the Romans trusted their army. After a conquest they were always careful to keep an army in the conquered country, but it was always a small army. If there was a big rebellion against Rome, more legions would march from Italy or from other provinces along the famous Roman roads. But as time went on, the Romans took the armies away from the countries inside the empire. They moved them to camps along the outside edges, or frontiers, of the empire. The proper job of the army was now to fight the wild tribes who lived outside the empire, across the rivers Rhine and Danube. A hundred years after the birth of Christ there was only one legion of 5,000 soldiers inside all Spain, France and Portugal. But there were four or five legions along the river Rhine. They were protecting the empire from the Germans who lived beyond the river.

If you were a boy or girl living in one of the Roman cities of France, you would probably never see a Roman soldier at all.

Britain was a bit different, because the Romans never bothered to finish off the job of conquering this out-of-the-way island. So they had to keep three legions watching the Welsh Britons in the West and the Picts and Scots in the North of Britain. But you would not see many soldiers in southern England or the Midlands, at London or at Roman Leicester. They were at their camps at Caerleon, Chester and York, or on duty along the great Roman Wall from Carlisle to Wallsend.

Because the Romans were not afraid of their subjects, they were able to trust them. The Romans did not even speak of 'subjects', but of 'friends and allies'. Yet these friends and allies were conquered peoples. The Romans trusted their subjects so much that they allowed Gauls and Britons and Spaniards to govern their own cities and villages. The Romans did not try to change the customs and laws of their subjects. The governors of the provinces just kept watch over the subjects from a distance. The subjects paid taxes and sent recruits to the Roman army. As long as they did this the Romans left them alone, to live as they liked. But it turned out that what the subjects liked to do was to copy the Roman way of life and to learn the Latin language which the Romans spoke. They wanted to read books in Latin and even to write books of their own in Latin. They wanted to build splendid buildings and to have fine towns just like Roman buildings and towns. They even wanted to go to school.

Before the Romans conquered them people like the Britons and Gauls were not naked savages or cannibals. They had some arts and crafts, but these were not very complicated. Everything that the Romans had or knew seemed better, and much more exciting, than their own things and ideas. Gauls and Britons thought that everything Roman was wonderful. They liked to wear Roman clothes and to have Roman names. They began to build Roman houses for themselves and Roman temples for their gods. They even bought Roman pottery from Italy and then copied it in their own workshops.

Perhaps the most surprising thing is that they began to speak Latin. The subjects of Rome did not really need to speak Latin unless they were in the Roman army. It was quite useful to   33

The remains of Roman houses in Leicester

speak Latin if a man fell into trouble. In the law courts the judges spoke Latin. But you could always hire a lawyer who knew Latin to defend you. There were two better reasons why the people in the provinces began to learn Latin. Some learned it because they wanted to become educated, and most books were in Latin. Other people learned it because they wanted to get on in the world. This usually meant joining the Roman army. The rich could become officers, and the poor, as we have seen, could become ordinary soldiers and then centurions. Another way of getting on was to be a lawyer. You had to know Latin very well indeed for that, and to have the best education. The third reason for learning Latin was the commonest of all. People just copied each other. They did not want to be left out of anything. They were afraid that other people would laugh at them if they could not speak the language of

34 Rome when everybody else could.

You may be surprised that Gauls and Britons, who were conquered peoples, could become officers in the Roman army. The Romans were very pleased when their subjects copied Roman customs and ways. If the Gauls served in the Roman army the Romans were ready to treat them as if they were true Romans, and to give them all the rights that belonged to the Romans of Italy. In this way the Gauls and Britons could become Roman citizens. The Romans liked to make Roman citizens of all sorts of people who helped them. The men who became mayors and councillors of towns in the provinces usually became Roman citizens like this. It was a way of keeping important and useful people in the conquered countries happy and loyal to Rome. But it was a new idea. Even the clever Greeks thought that a man could not belong to two places. The Romans just did not see why a man should not be a citizen of London, live there and perhaps be mayor of London, and at the same time be a Roman and think of the emperor as his king. This is quite an easy idea for us. Yet nobody thought of it before the Romans.

The Roman Emperor Claudius was famous for wanting to turn his subjects into Roman citizens. People in Italy laughed at him because he once said: 'I think that Greeks and Britons and Spaniards and Africans and Gauls should all be Romans. I want to see all the people in the world wearing *togas*.' Why did he want to see them all wearing togas? It was because, as we shall find on page 51, only Romans were allowed to wear the dress called a toga. Claudius was not in a hurry about this. The Romans, like the British, were never in a hurry to make changes. But all the same they made them in the end. Once Claudius made a speech about the Gauls. A copy of it was found in the great city of Lyons, which the Romans called Lugdunum, in the middle of France. He said: 'The Gauls fought Julius Caesar for ten years, but since then they have obeyed us for a hundred years. They backed Rome up against the Germans in the German wars. They are very rich people, and I should like to see them marrying Romans and becoming Romans. That is much better than keeping themselves to themselves.' 35

5 Discovering Roman Towns

We know a lot about the Roman towns because some of them still exist in ruins today. When they were destroyed at the end of the Roman Empire, rivers often covered their ruins in mud several feet deep. This kept the ruins safe for hundreds of years. In recent times people have discovered these ruins and dug them out again. In England we have a ruined Roman town called Verulamium, at St Albans in Hertfordshire, which you can visit. Sometimes, too, the shape of ruins underneath the soil has been seen from airplanes.

Some Roman cities were gradually pulled down and rebuilt by the people who lived in them in later ages. Often a few Roman buildings remain in use in old towns today. Part of the fort at Richborough on the Straits of Dover is still standing. So is a bit of the old Roman wall of London in the street still called London Wall. A Roman temple was found underneath a big London office that had been destroyed by bombs in an air-raid.

The most famous ruin of a Roman city is Pompeii, near Naples, in Italy. The *volcano* Vesuvius buried this town deep in dust and ashes in a single day. It was 24 August, AD 79. No trace of it was left, though it was a big town. We shall read on page 68 an account of how this disaster happened, written by someone who watched from far off. Most of the folk who lived in Pompeii were smothered where they stood. About two hundred years ago the Italians began to dig Pompeii up again. Below the soil they found houses, markets, shops and temples still standing, as on the day of their disaster. Roofs and walls had often collapsed. Many had caught fire before the dust

A dining room at Pompeii, with stone seats and table

buried them. In some the furniture was still there in the rooms. Fine statues stood in the streets, or lay where they had fallen when the earth shook and quaked. Splendid pictures, painted on plaster, still covered the walls of the parlours and dining rooms of the finest houses. Plates and cups and the remains of food still covered the tables. Everywhere lay the bones and skeletons of the people of Pompeii who perished on that fatal day, as they tried unsuccessfully to escape.

The people who lived in these towns used to put up notices, which we call *inscriptions*. These were cut in stone on the statues and tombstones of well-known men. Often soldiers would club together to put up notices in memory of a dead friend or a popular officer. These notices, or inscriptions, are in Latin. They tell the story of men's lives. They give the man's name, his trade, and all the posts or jobs that he held. Here is one

about a man from a small town in the Alps. In English it goes
like this:

IN HONOUR OF AURELIUS MAXULUS

HE WAS KIND AND GENEROUS TO EVERYBODY
HE GAVE OUR TOWN FREE BREAD IN TIME OF FAMINE
HE REPAIRED OUR WATER SUPPLY WHEN THE PIPES HAD ALL
BROKEN DOWN.

The mayor of a city in Spain turns up in another inscription:

IN HONOUR OF LUCIUS LUCRETIUS

HE WAS TOWN COUNCILLOR, MAYOR AND CHIEF PRIEST OF THE CITY
HE GAVE US A CIRCUS AND BEAST SHOW LASTING FOUR DAYS
HE GAVE US CHARIOT RACES FREE
HE GAVE ALL THE CITIZENS OF OUR TOWN A FREE BANQUET.

Sometimes the town council set out its rules and orders
on stone slabs in the market place. Everyone could see and
read them there. As there were no newspapers and no television
this was the only way of telling everyone what the council
had decided.

At election times people used to scribble on the walls all over
the town, like this: 'Primus the laundryman wants Lucius
Ceius to be mayor.' Or, 'Make Bruttius Balbus mayor. He won't
waste our money.' 'Vote for Casellius and Albucius to be
Keepers of the Market. We need men like them in the city.'
'The farmers want Casellius to be mayor.' Sometimes men
used to attack their rivals rather cleverly: 'All the drunkards
want Cerrinius to be mayor', or 'The thieves want you to vote
for Vatia'. You can still read inscriptions like this on the walls
of Pompeii. We learn a great deal about life in the Roman
towns from them.

TOWN PLANNING

The Romans planned their towns carefully. As you approached
the town on the main road you would pass through a great
Arch of Triumph. On its walls were carved pictures showing

An Arch of Triumph across a street in Rome

the victories of the emperor. Next you reached the city wall, and passed through a splendid gateway.

In the centre of the town there was always a town square, or *forum*. This was the place where the citizens met and elected the mayors and officials of the cities. Around it you would find the town hall, where the town council met, the law court, where the judges heard disputes, and the temples of the Roman gods. A town would often have a small public library, and there was always a market building. Often there was a covered terrace, or a long shelter, where people could sit in the shade in summer and talk together. Somewhere in the town there would certainly be a Roman theatre. The streets of a Roman town were straight, and crossed at right angles. They were 39

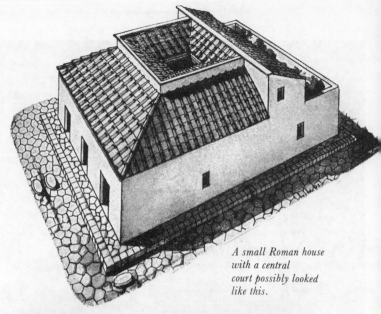

A small Roman house with a central court possibly looked like this.

The central court of a great house at Herculaneum

narrow, but there were no wriggling little lanes going in every direction, such as you find in old English cities.

HOUSES

The most surprising thing about the houses is that there were no gardens, and very few windows that looked on the streets. The houses were built round small square courtyards, and the windows looked out on the courtyards. This was to keep the rooms shady and cool in the long, hot Italian summers. A small Roman house looked like the picture here, which shows the house of a middle-class person. Poorer people lived in one or two rooms in big buildings like our blocks of flats. But a rich man's house, like the house in the picture opposite might have two or three courtyards with rooms round each. It is at Herculaneum, another town buried by the volcano. The rooms had no fireplaces and no chimneys. The Romans kept their houses warm in winter by means of a kind of central-heating called a *hypocaust*. This means 'hot underneath'. Hot air from a furnace passed through pipes in the walls and the floor. You can see hypocausts in most Roman houses found in Britain. The Romans found Britain a very cold country

A mosaic from Pompeii of a watch dog.

41

after Italy, and could not do without their hypocausts, just as many of us have central heating in our houses today.

The floors had no carpets. They were covered with *mosaics*. These are patterns or pictures made out of thousands of tiny coloured stones, set in concrete. Some of the pictures in this book are of Roman mosaics. The mosaic on page 41 shows the guard dog of a Roman house.

SHOPS AND MARKETS

There were plenty of shops in Roman towns. Often a room in a private house was cut off from the rest of the house, and used as a shop, opening on to the street. Then there were the enclosed markets. These were groups of stalls built round a courtyard. Sometimes there was a fountain of water in the middle of the courtyard. Each market was for one kind of shop only. One market was for butchers, a second for bakers, a third

A relief on a wall showing customers buying pillows

for grocers or drapers. This must have made shopping easy. The stalls were quite small. The shopkeeper stood behind a stone slab on which he laid his wares. Sometimes there were huge jars in the slab, to hold flour or wine or olive oil. Look at this view of a shop in Pompeii and imagine that the shopkeepers are standing there, or that you are buying a pillow like these people.

THE GODS AND THE RULERS OF THE TOWNS

We have mentioned mayors and town councillors. These were people living in the towns and villages who looked after them, just as your town or county council looks after the place where you live. The people of each town elected mayors and judges every year to govern the place. Just as Rome had two consuls, so each town always had two mayors, instead of just one. The two kept watch on each other. If one tried to steal the town's money, the second mayor would stop him. When anything needed doing in the town, such as building a new theatre, the two mayors had to agree about it, or nothing could be done. They also had to take the advice of the town council, which kept watch over both mayors. So it was quite hard for the mayors to cheat or rob the town.

The people did not elect the town councillors. The mayors became town councillors for life after their year of office, just as the consuls of Rome became senators for life; for the towns liked to copy Rome as much as possible. Every man wanted to become mayor and councillor of his town. For this he did not need to be very rich, but there was a rule that no one could become a town councillor unless he owned a certain amount of property, such as a farm of twelve to sixteen hectares. So they were usually men of the middle class. They might be merchants or shopkeepers or retired officers from the army.

The town councils and the mayors were very useful to the Roman emperor. The empire was very big. The emperor and the governors of provinces could not keep an eye on everything. The town councils and mayors ran their town and all the countryside belonging to it. They even collected taxes for the emperor, and sent the money to Rome. They had their own

43

police and fire brigades too. So the emperor was saved a lot of trouble and could get on with his own work. But sometimes the town councils had difficulties which they could not manage by themselves. Then they wrote to the emperor and asked for his advice and help. The Emperor Vespasian, who ruled after the death of Nero, once wrote this to the little town of Sabora in Spain.

> Since I hear that your city is in great difficulties, I will allow you to move the town down from the hill top and rebuild it on the flat ground. You may keep for the town the taxes which you have always collected, but you may not raise new taxes unless you first ask the governor of your province for permission.

On page 87 you can read how the governor Pliny tried to help the cities of Bithynia.

Around the town square there were the temples of the chief gods. Religion in ancient times was very unlike religion today. The Romans were not Jews or Muslims or Christians. We should call them *pagans*. The Romans knew about the religion of the Jews, but did not like it very much. Jesus Christ lived early in the history of the Roman Empire, and in the next hundred years only a few people were Christians. Mohammed did not live till the end of the Roman Empire. Romans believed that there were many spirits and gods which controlled the life of men. It was wise to keep all these spirits as happy and friendly as possible.

You could do this by making offerings of food and praying to them. They also thought of these spirits as if they were mysterious persons who could appear in human shape. Jupiter, the god of the sky, whom they called 'Greatest and Best', protected the Roman nation. Then there was Juno his wife, and Minerva, who had to do with all the skill and craft of workmen in daily life, and Mars, the god of war and soldiers.

These spirits were so important that the Roman nobles acted as their special priests. But these priests were not clergymen 44 or parsons. They were ordinary politicians and statesmen.

It was their duty to see that the proper offerings were given to the gods of Rome in the city of Rome. It was not necessary for other people to attend at the offerings. There was nothing like church services, and there were no congregations or parishes. Each family had its own family gods, who had to have offerings like the big gods. It was the duty of the head of each family to see that these offerings were made. At meal times people usually poured out a few drops of wine for the god of the household to drink; in return they believed that he would protect all the family.

It was the same in each town of the Roman Empire. Each one had to help look after the big gods, but it would also have some special gods of its own. Each god had to have his own temple and statue and meals. Some of the city councillors had to take on the job of being priests and looking after the gods of the city. Otherwise they thought that a disaster would hit the city, such as an earthquake or a flood or a *famine* or a plague

A Roman temple at Nîmes in France

of illness. In later times the Christians refused to have anything to do with the pagan gods. This made the people who were not Christians very angry. If any disaster happened to the city they would say that it was all the fault of the Christians. They said that the Christians had annoyed the city gods, and the gods were punishing the city. The result would be that the Christians were dragged before the nearest Roman governor, who usually ordered them to be put to death. After a few weeks the excitement would end, and the Christians would carry on as usual until the next disaster.

Roman temples were not a bit like our churches. People did not come to sit and pray inside them. Really they were just the houses of the gods. A temple was a big room, built rather grandly, with a porch and a row of pillars. There was a statue of the god inside, and an altar outside.

In this picture you can see men bringing animals to be sacrificed at an altar. That was all there was in Roman religon: you made your offering at the altar, and spoke a prayer out loud, so that god could hear, asking him to protect you in return for your presents. Later on, more and more Romans became Christians, because the old religion did not mean much to them.

6 Day to Day Life in Roman Towns

FOOD AND COSTUME

As there was no gas or electricity or paraffin to give good light, the Romans usually got up at dawn and went to bed at sunset. In southern countries like Italy the summer days are never so long as in Britain, and the winter days are not as short as in an English winter. In the hot summer of Italy the morning hours are the best time for work. Most people started very early and stopped work about midday. At night they could burn oil, made from the olive fruit, in small lamps made of pottery. The wick was stuck into a hole like a spout. But olive oil gave a very weak light and was rather expensive to burn, so they thought it rather wasteful, even wicked, to stay up reading or talking by lamp-light. All shows were in day-light and out of doors: the theatres and amphitheatres had no roofs.

Most Romans did not eat any breakfast. Their first meal was about midday when the real work of the day was over. The chief meal was four hours later. This was a big dinner with several different things to eat. Some families had only this one meal a day, and ate very heartily. How would you like to wait all day for your food? You would probably find Roman food rather dull and even nasty. Things do not keep fresh for long in the warm climate of Italy. Bread was very coarse and black. The dry summer of Italy burnt up the grass, so cows gave little milk. Romans used the milk of goats and sheep instead, and made strong smelly cheese out of it. Instead of butter they used olive oil. There was some fruit in late summer, but there was no jam and no sweets, because there was no sugar; they did not grow sugar cane or sugar beet, but used honey 47

Two Roman lamps. The duck, from Pompeii, is made of bronze, the other is made of clay.

instead. Tea, coffee and cocoa plants did not grow in the inhabited world, so they drank wine. There was plenty of this, because grapes grow as freely as blackberries in Mediterranean lands. They often mixed their wine with water, as we do with orange juice.

Rich people ate meat and fish in large quantities. But meat was expensive and tough in the hot South, and fish kept fresh only for a day.

Working people ate mostly bread and other things made of flour, like spaghetti, and goat's-cheese, olive oil and wine. They could only have fresh fruit, salads and vegetables for a short time in the year because of the dry summers. Perhaps the things you would miss most would be butter, sweets, cakes, oranges and bananas, and ice-cream. Ice was a great luxury. Huge blocks of it were fetched from the high mountains in winter and stored in cellars. But only the very rich could afford to have ice in their drinks.

Roman clothes were most peculiar. They did not wear coats and trousers, or skirts and blouses and dresses. The Celts (the people who lived in France and Britain) wore trousers, but

48

the Romans looked down on them. It was an insult to call a man a 'trouser-wearer'. Instead the men wore a tunic indoors and a toga out of doors, on top of it. A tunic was a fairly close-fitting shirt which hung down to your knees. The toga was a great piece of woollen cloth, cut in a half circle, about six metres long and two metres wide. You wound this round your body, and over your shoulders, and under your arms, and pinned it together with a sort of big safety-pin. It was supposed to hang in graceful folds, but it prevented you from

Part of a relief showing Romans in togas studying a book

moving about suddenly or quickly. It was very awkward, like wearing a blanket. When doing hard work or exercise the Romans took their togas off. Would you feel comfortable, dressed like the people in togas in the picture?

These clothes were of plain materials, with no patterns or colours, unless you were a nobleman. Then you had a purple stripe round the edge of your tunic or toga. The dresses of ladies were much the same. But their togas were cut square and could be coloured. City folk did not wear hats, neither men nor women. Fashion must have been much duller for ladies than nowadays. But they made up for this by wearing lots of different rings, bangles, necklaces and jewels of all sorts. They were very fussy about their hair, and had many different ways of doing it.

Boys wearing tunics take presents to a wedding

The Romans often grew tired of their togas. They preferred the tunics, and took to wearing better shaped and more comfortable clothes from foreign countries. They liked the roomy loose kind of tunic, called a 'Dalmatic', from the Roman province of Dalmatia. In this sculpture on the opposite page two boys wearing tunics are taking presents to a wedding party. But the toga was the proper dress of a Roman citizen. You were not allowed to wear one unless you were a Roman citizen, and the emperors tried to force citizens to wear their togas in public. It was like wearing a school cap or uniform. If you had no toga on people would say that you were naked, even if you had a tunic from neck to knees.

AMUSEMENTS AND COMFORTS

There were plenty of amusements in Roman towns. Of course you could not see a show every day, but there were always shows on holidays, and there were plenty of holidays. On the feast-days of the different gods, on the emperor's birthday or on his *coronation* day, there was always something to see. Often there were plays. These were what the Romans called 'panto-mimes', which were more like musicals than what we call pantomimes. The story was told in music with songs and dances. But people looked forward most to the horse races, the beast shows and the gladiators. Perhaps you have seen a film of Roman horse races.

The jockey rider stood in a little car drawn by two or four fast horses, as our picture on the next page shows. These were harnessed in a line abreast. Four teams at a time went round a course rather like a dirt-track or dog-track, as fast as they could go, in a circus or *amphitheatre*. The fun came when they tried to pass at the corners.

In the beast shows men fought wild animals. It was rather like a Spanish bull fight. But the greatest thrill came from the 'games'. Here men fought men with spears and swords until one of them killed the other. The Romans called them *gladiators*. It was a good deal more blood-thirsty than boxing or all-in wrestling. In the picture on the next page you can see how

gladiators fought even when wounded, with spears sticking into their legs, and how they held their shields.

These shows took place in big stone theatres and amphitheatres. The theatres were shaped in a half circle and were open to the sky. Rows and rows of seats rose from the ground to a great height. The stage had no curtain: it was just a stone platform. The back wall, built to look like a big Roman house, was the only scenery.

The amphitheatres were like big football stadiums—the word means 'double theatres'. Like the theatres they were usually built of stone, very large and impressive. They might hold 100,000 people. Some still exist, and are used for pageants and games, and in Spain and France even for bull fights. The most famous is the Colosseum at Rome. Small towns sometimes had a little amphitheatre dug out of the ground, with seats of wood. There is one built in this way, which you can visit at Silchester, near Reading.

Look at the picture of a Roman amphitheatre on the next page, and imagine yourself there on a hot day. You go in by the great archways, and then find yourself in a place like this. The wild beasts will be driven in through the tall doorway at one end, and the fighters will come in from all around the floor. Then the excitement begins.

Everybody went to the races and the 'games'. Famous jockeys and gladiators were as popular as film stars and pop singers today. Educated people sometimes looked down their noses at the races, but they went just the same. The Roman senator Pliny objected to the betting and the rivalry that took place. He said:

> It is very odd that tens of thousands of people should want to watch horses galloping and men in cars. If they went for the speed of the horses or the skill of the riders, there

Opposite above: *This relief shows a racing chariot turning round the course markers at great speed*

Opposite below: *A mosaic of gladiators fighting at the games*

might be something in it. But they only cheer the coloured shirt. If you changed the jockeys' shirts round in the middle of a race, they would cheer just as loudly for the other chap. Why, I have even seen senators and important people cheering for their colour.

If there was no theatre show, no races, and no games, how did an idle townsman pass the afternoon? He went to the baths. Every town had its baths, and often they were very grand. They were a mixture of baths and sports club. And the Romans went to them as we go to the coffee-bar or the pub round the corner, to the cricket club and the bowling green. The richer Romans had baths in their houses, but they liked to go to the public baths to take exercise, to meet their friends, and to gossip and watch other people. There were changing rooms and lounges, and a set of bathing halls, with cold, warm and hot water, and a great central court for sunbathing and exercise. People did not swim in the baths. They were too small and too shallow. You will notice this if you visit the famous Roman bath which still exists at the city of Bath in Somerset. The baths were very cheap. Everybody went, rich and poor, men and women. But some emperors forbade mixed bathing.

Strangers from distant parts of the empire always admired two things above all in Roman towns: the water supply and the drains. The Romans were good engineers, though most of their engineering had to be done in stone and brick and concrete, where we use iron and steel. They built water mains, or *aqueducts*, many miles long, to bring water to their cities. The water flowed along a pipe that was nearly level. When they came to a valley they built bridges with hundreds of arches to carry the pipes. In Britain aqueducts were not often needed, because water can usually be found everywhere in rivers or wells. But in the long dry summers of Italy, southern France and Spain it seemed like a miracle to have water flowing at

Opposite above: *The stage of a Roman theatre in Tunisia*

Opposite below: *The amphitheatre at Pompeii*

The aqueduct near Nimes in France
Opposite: *The Roman bathing pool at Bath*

public taps; it was even laid on to private houses in the towns.

Water-pipes, drains and lavatories go together. In Roman towns there were drains laid along all the streets, to carry off the rain and sewage. There were plenty of public lavatories too, with neat stone seats, and even a hand-basin. At Rome itself, which was a huge city, the sewers were very large, and drained into the river Tiber. A friend of the Emperor Augustus once had himself rowed through the sewers in·a boat. These drains must have been very smelly. Even the Romans could not bring enough water to wash out the sewers. But their drains were a great deal better than nothing. With theatres, baths, markets, paved streets, water-mains and drains, the Roman towns were still not nearly so comfortable and clean as a modern British town. But they were much better than any that existed between then and now. After the end of the Roman Empire it was 1,500 years before the ordinary working people in towns were able to enjoy anything like the comfort and amusements of Roman times again—to get a bath easily, to drink clean water, to walk in clean streets and to go and see a splendid show cheaply.

57

7 Education

It was much more difficult to get an education in Roman times than nowadays. There were no free schools, and there were no schools at all in the countryside, only in the towns. Yet a great number of poor people managed to learn to read and write. Lots of letters have been found in Egypt. Quite ordinary people, such as farmers and shopkeepers and soldiers, wrote them to their families. Even in towns there were no big schools in fine buildings. with hundreds of pupils, such as there are in Britain today. A Roman school was a place where one master taught twenty or thirty pupils. It was not in a special house. It might be just a place under a big archway near the town square. The only furniture was a number of benches and flat desks. Anyone could start a school, as long as he could get pupils to come and pay. But schooling did not cost very much. Usually each pupil would pay his teacher four Roman silver pennies a month, but if the teacher was famous he would get a lot more. They usually asked as much as they thought they could get.

Yet the teaching was not really so very different from today. There were three kinds of school. First of all, from seven to twelve years old, the Romans learned writing, reading and arithmetic. Next, from twelve to fourteen years old, they learned what they called 'grammar'. This meant reading famous books, and having lessons about them. They read the plays and poems and histories written by the great writers of Greece and Rome. In this way they learned what we call history and literature and languages. The Romans did not bother with any foreign languages except Greek. This second period of schooling was like our secondary schools. But there was no science, and nobody had to pass any examinations.

The third period of Roman schooling was more like going to a college or *university*. Very clever professors gave classes and lectures to young men who had finished their 'grammar'. It must have been rather like listening to the more difficult talks on the radio or television. Sometimes pupils had to make speeches about the things they had learned in the classes. They did this instead of writing exercises or essays. People

A relief showing boys in school reading to their teacher

spent more of their time learning how to make speeches than we do. You had to be able to talk 'like a book', and not just in everyday language. This skill in talking was called *oratory*. Even in your town council no one would listen to you unless you were a good *orator*. So Romans spent a lot of time learning how to do it.

BOOKS

Instead of paper the Romans used a stuff made from reeds and called *papyrus*. It looked rather like coarse paper and was light brown in colour. They did not cut it up into little sheets and make square books out of it. They used it in very long narrow strips, and wound these up into a roll very like a toilet roll. You wrote in short columns of lines. To read a roll, you unrolled a bit at a time and held it in both hands. You had to roll up what you had read as you went on. It was very awkward. No wonder the Romans often preferred hearing a speech to reading a roll. For writing something short, and for school work, they used small wooden boards. These were covered with wax which they scratched with a pointed rod. In time they began to use sheets of skin, called *parchment*, and invented the book by binding these sheets together. But all the Greek and Latin writers wrote their great books on rolls of papyrus. Bookmakers made one copy at a time by hand and sold them in shops. Books were expensive and valuable.

Romans did not read their books to themselves. They read them aloud. Rich men had servants whose job it was to read aloud to their masters. Often the servants read aloud during the long Roman dinners. Augustine, the Roman bishop who wrote a diary about 1,500 years ago, was astonished once to see somebody who was reading without making any sound. It was so odd that Augustine wrote it down in his diary. As far as we know that was the first time that anyone ever read to himself. See the pictures on pages 49 and 59.

WRITERS

The Romans learned from the Greeks how to write books. At first they just copied what the Greeks wrote and put it into their own language, Latin. But they soon began to write books of their own. They wrote histories about their own country, plays about Roman people, and poems of all sorts. The Romans were very fond of writing history, because they were proud of all the wars they had won, and of all the lands they ruled. They wanted everyone else to know about them. The great general Julius Caesar wrote his own account of how he had beaten the Gauls and conquered their country, France. No wonder that we know so much about the Romans.

The Romans were not quite so good at thinking up new ideas and making up stories. Most of their stories were about history. Instead of fairy-stories and adventure stories they used to tell children about famous soldiers and heroes. These were some of the stories that they told.

'How three Romans beat the Etruscan army'

'How the geese saved Rome from the Gauls'

'How Coriolanus became a traitor'

'How Regulus kept his promise to the enemy'

Virgil, who lived just before the birth of Christ, wrote the most famous of all Latin poems. It is a story in verse called 'The Tale of Aeneas'. Even this was a kind of history. It tells about a man called Aeneas (pronounced 'Eenyass'). He wandered with a band of friends over the seas, in a ship looking for Italy. At last, after many adventures, he found Italy and built a tiny city. This became the home of the earliest and first Romans of all. Aeneas beat his enemies and married a princess called Lavinia. Most Romans knew much of the tale of Aeneas by heart. Many poets in different countries have used the tale of Aeneas as a model for their own poems. One of these was the great English poet Milton. From reading Virgil's poem he learned how to plan and write his own long poem, which is called 'Paradise Lost'.

8 Work in the World of Rome

People work in order to buy clothes and food, and to pay for rooms or a house to live in. Everything else is less necessary. Life would not be so pleasant, perhaps, but we could still live without such things as toys and bicycles, watches and television sets. In Roman days most people were busy in the countryside growing food, or plants and animals from which they made cloth. Just a few people were busy in towns making luxuries like jewellery, scent and furniture. As there were no machines, the workmen made everything by hand. There were no big businesses. People who made things did not earn much more money than those who grew things. Those who sold things made more than those who grew them or made them. The shopkeeper nearly always comes off best. But we do not often hear of Roman traders and shopkeepers becoming millionaires.

The rich man in Roman times was usually someone who owned a lot of farm land. Crops and harvests are not so reliable in the dry Mediterranean weather as in rainy Britain. If you had a lot of farm land you could store up the spare corn and sell it at a high price another season, when all the crops failed and people were starving. In Roman times if your own harvest was bad you would be very hungry until the next year's harvest was ready. No wonder that the big landowners were the richest and most important people in the country. No wonder that most people worked on the land.

Many craftsmen, such as potters and shoemakers, worked in their own small rooms by themselves. They would make enough shoes or pots to buy food and clothing for their families. Sometimes a richer man would hire a few craftsmen. They would work together in a workshop, and so make more things. But there were no machines. So the workshops never became factories. Sometimes the workmen were slaves who belonged to the owner of the workshop. The owners of slaves made more money than the others, because they could make a slave work longer and harder than a hired man. But they had to buy their slaves and train them. That cost money too. So there were always plenty of free men working for hire as well as slaves, in the workshops.

Here is a picture of a Roman bakery. It comes from the carvings on a rich baker's tomb at Rome. Look at the workers mixing the bread by hand, and taking it to the oven.

TRANSPORT

Later on we will read how the Romans travelled along their great roads and highways (pages 83-6). But it was much cheaper to send goods by sea and by river than by road. So there were plenty of sailors and sea-traders. Horses and oxen and wagons wear out much more quickly, and carry far less, than ships and barges with big, roomy holds. (Look at the huge barrels this little boat is carrying; it is pictured on a stone *sculpture*

from France.) Besides, animals need food, and sailing ships do not. The Roman Empire was all round the Mediterranean sea, and big rivers like the Rhine and Danube, the Rhone and the Nile, ran through it. So often the quickest way to get from one part to another was by water. As the Mediterranean sea is often very calm and windless in summer most ships, big and small, carried oars. When the wind fell the crews had to start lugging at the oars. This also helped them to escape from pirates; there were quite a number of pirates lurking in odd corners of the Mediterranean, though the Romans kept fleets to catch them. We have many pictures of Roman trading ships from Pompeii and from North Africa. There were many kinds, from small rowing boats for fishing, to sailing ships for carrying cargoes, seen in this mosaic from Africa.

THE PRIVATE LIFE OF THE WORKERS

We know a lot about the life of the free craftsmen of the Roman world, because like everyone else, as we have seen, they often set up stone inscriptions about themselves. They formed clubs of their own, one for each trade. The members paid subscriptions, and every month they held a club dinner. Each club had its own special god, like the patron saint of a church club today. When a member died the club paid for his funeral out of the club money. The clubs had their own treasurer, who looked after the money, and a chairman or president, whom they elected each year. Some had a priest to look after the club god. The club of the carpenters at Rome had its own doctor. This was an ordinary member who was good at 'first aid' –washing wounds and tying up broken legs. In the rules of a club we find that:

> Whoever wants to join the club must pay four hundred pennies and a big jar of wine as an entrance fee, and five pennies a month afterwards.
> If a member dies without paying his pennies for six months the club will not pay for his funeral.

Opposite: *A mosaic showing ships sailing past a light-house*

If the treasurer does not obey the chairman he must pay a big jar of wine as a punishment.

If anyone swears at the priest or hits him, he must pay a fine of two pennies.

So it cost less to be rude to the priest than to the chairman. These Roman pennies were worth much more than our pennies. They were copper coins called 'asses'; sixteen of them went to a Roman 'silver penny', or 'denarius'. The Romans also had a fourpenny piece called a 'sesterce'. Most workmen were paid no more than a silver penny a day. That gives you some idea of how much the club cost. You had to subscribe about four days' pay a year. It would take a fair time to save up the four hundred pennies, or twenty-five days' pay, for the entry fee. But you got it all back later on. It went to pay for your club dinners and your own funeral when you were dead!

How could a man live and keep a family on a 'silver penny' a day? Only because food and clothes were much cheaper than today. A Roman soldier got 300 silver pennies a year. His food only cost him 80 a year; he paid 60 silver pennies for a year's bread, and 20 for everything else.

But it was not always holidays in ancient times. Here we see a man and boy hard at work making things of copper, hammering and carving. You can see some of the tools he uses and the boy who helps him.

9 Pliny: A Roman Nobleman

We have seen in the chapter about towns what a lot we can learn about the life of ordinary people who lived in the Roman Empire from stone inscriptions. But we know most about the life of rich people because they wrote books and letters. One of the Romans about whom we know most is a man called Pliny the Younger. There is a collection of his letters in which he describes his life and work. He tells his friends about the news of Rome and tells stories about his friends and his enemies, and about other famous people.

Pliny lived from AD 62 to about 110. His father was a rich landowner, and his uncle, Pliny the Elder, had been an officer in the Roman army and navy. When Pliny was a young man of eighteen he was living with his uncle near the sea in south Italy. His uncle was the admiral of a Roman fleet which was kept at the port of Misenum, near the modern city of Naples, and only about 30 kilometres from the little mountain of Vesuvius. This was an old volcano, which had never given any trouble as long as the Romans could remember. One day there was a frightful explosion. It was as if an atomic bomb had exploded. The volcano had woken up and blown its top off. Young Pliny tells what happened.

> For many days before there had been earthquakes. We did not mind them. We are used to them in these parts. But that night they got so bad that we thought the earth was turning upside down. My mother rushed into my room. I got up and we sat outside the house, near the seashore. At dawn we could see that the sea had disappeared. Fish had

were lying on the dry land. Then a huge black cloud appeared. Tongues of fire shot out of it like flashes of lightning, but much worse. Ashes began to fall on us, but not very thickly. Behind us blackness began to cover the whole land. It became darker than night. It was like being shut up in a room without any light. We could hear people shouting and shrieking and howling.

That was what it was like 30 kilometres away from the volcano. His uncle, the admiral, took some ships and crossed the bay to rescue people from close to Vesuvius. They found that the wind was so strong that they could not get off again. They were caught between the volcano and the sea. Pliny tells us about it:

My uncle tried to cheer them up, and to make them feel safer he ordered baths to be got ready. After he had had his bath he took his dinner.

This was rather like the Englishman, Francis Drake, who played bowls while the Spanish fleet was sailing up the Channel to attack England. We saw on page 55 that the baths were the chief amusement of the Romans. Pliny goes on:

Sheets of flame could be seen on the slopes of Vesuvius. My uncle pretended that these were farm houses set on fire by accident, from which the owners had fled. Then he went to bed, but ashes and dust fell so thickly that they nearly blocked the doorways up. So he got up and left the house. To protect themselves from the falling dust and stones, they all tied pillows on their heads with bits of sheets. The flames came nearer. There was a smell of sulphur. My uncle staggered along leaning on the arms of two servants. Next morning he was found dead on the shore.

The same great clouds of dust and ashes that day buried the city of Pompeii many metres deep. It was not discovered again until people began to dig it up two hundred years ago.

Young Pliny escaped from the danger. He was finishing his education at the time. He became a lawyer and then a senator, and he held many big jobs in the service of the emperor. For some years he was head of the office which looked after the money of the Roman Empire and collected the taxes. He found this work rather boring sometimes, and said: 'I am busy with a big but tiresome job. I sit in court to settle disputes. I make up the accounts of money. I write a lot of very dull business letters.' He was more interested in his work as a lawyer. Several times he took part in big trials. He helped to accuse Roman governors who had been cruel to the people whom they had been governing. He was very proud of the fact that the people asked for him specially to do this work. 'The people of Spain want to accuse the governor Classicus. They have asked the Senate to name me to be their lawyer. The Senate has decided to appoint me if I will agree. It is a great honour.' The cases were very long. Once the Emperor was in court when Pliny was making a speech. He tells us: 'The Emperor was very worried about me. He thought that I was getting so excited that I would make myself ill. So he sent me a message asking me to be careful.'

The truth is that Pliny thought a lot of himself. He was rather a conceited man. Perhaps the emperor only meant that Pliny's speech was too long, and he had better stop!

Another time Pliny tells us: 'Yesterday in court the place was crowded out with people listening. A well-dressed young chap had his tunic torn to rags in the crush, and stood listening to me with only his toga on, for seven hours. I was speaking for seven hours.' No wonder the emperor got tired, if Pliny's speeches were as long as that.

There was a famous lawyer called Regulus, whom Pliny hated. Regulus had been a favourite of the Emperor Domitian, who had been very cruel and unpopular. After the death of Domitian, Pliny writes:

Have you ever seen anyone so scared as Regulus since the death of Domitian? He did a lot of wrong in Domitian's reign, and now he is afraid I may get him punished. So I will if I can. He has fairly got the wind up. But he is rich and has a lot of friends, and many people are frightened of him. But I might manage to ruin him all the same.

The Roman nobles were always quarrelling among themselves like this. In the end Pliny did nothing about Regulus. Then Regulus died, and Pliny wrote this about him: 'I often look for Regulus in court, and almost wish he was there. He was very keen on his work, and took a lot of trouble. However he has done a good job by dying. Pity he did not die sooner!'

Mostly Pliny writes about his friends. The senator Spurinna had been a general in command of an army on the Rhine next to Germany. Pliny tells us:

Yesterday the Senate voted that a statue should be set up in honour of Spurinna. The emperor himself suggested it. Often other men get honours who have never seen a battle or heard a trumpet except at the theatre. But Spurinna won his honours by blood and sweat. He marched into the land of the Germans, and made them do what the Romans wanted.

In Pliny's letters we can see how Romans tried to get good jobs in the service of the emperor. He often wrote to his friends to get posts for young men who were starting their life's work. Once he wrote to a man who was probably governor of Britain:

Dear Priscus, you are always glad to help me, and I am glad to do the same for you. You are in command of a big army, and have plenty of jobs which you can give to chaps. You have had time to help all your own friends. Now help one of mine. It is Voconius that I mean. He comes from a good family, and has just been Chief Priest in Spain. We were at school together, and he is one of my best friends. He is very clever and amusing. Give him the best job you can and make a friend of him.

This is one of the ways in which the Romans managed things in the government. You could not get very far in the army or in the civil service unless you had a useful friend to help you along. Notice that Pliny did not bother to say whether Voconius was good at the job! He just said that he was a pleasant man.

Pliny often tells us how he treated his slaves and servants. Rich Romans had many slaves who were their own property. But they were not usually cruel to them. They let the slaves have pocket money, and treated them as servants and workmen. Often Romans set their slaves free in return for good work. They were then called 'freedmen'. They often continued to work for the same master when they were free. But sometimes they set up a little workshop or opened a shop with the savings from their pocket money. When a freedman called Zosimus fell ill Pliny wrote about him:

> Dear Paulinus, I must take special care of Zosimus. He is honest, loyal and clever. He is a trained actor. He plays the *lyre* well. He is splendid at reading aloud. I am very fond of him. He used to cough terribly. So I sent him for a long holiday to Egypt. He seemed better, but now he is ill again. So I want to send him to your country-house in the south of France. The fresh air and the milk in those parts is good for cases of this kind.

In his own house Pliny always gave the same food and wine to his freedmen as he had at his own table. This surprised his friends and guests, but he said at dinner: 'I think my freedmen are not my servants but my guests. It does not cost so much to feed them decently if you don't always have the most expensive things yourself. I just eat what they eat.'

Another time Pliny writes about the death of some of his servants:

> I am so upset about the death and illness of some of my young freedmen and slaves. But I cheer myself up by remembering that I am so quick to set them free from slavery. Besides I allow my slaves to make *wills* of their own,

and to leave their pocket money and savings to their friends. But I expect these friends to be freedmen or slaves belonging to my household.

Not all Romans would do as much as this. Most owners of slaves expected to keep all the savings of their slaves for themselves when the slaves died. Pliny adds: 'I know that most people think that the death of their slaves is like the loss of valuable animals, and nothing more. People who think that are hardly human.'

It was not wise to be too harsh to your slaves. Pliny tells us what happened to the cruel Macedo:

My dear Acilius, the slaves of Macedo have done a frightful thing. He was a proud and cruel master. When he was at bath in his country house, his slaves suddenly surrounded him. One hit him in the neck, another in the face. They kicked him all over, and when they thought he was dead they threw him on the boiler-top to make sure. He kept still, and they left him for dead. Some loyal slaves rescued him, and he came to his senses. He did not live long, but he lasted till he saw his slaves punished.

Pliny was frightened by this story. He adds: 'See what dangers surround you. You can't be safe by being kind and easy to your slaves. They will murder you out of sheer wickedness.' Yet we never hear of slaves murdering kind masters. The Roman law punished slaves very severely if they attacked their masters. All the slaves who lived in the house were put to death. But the Roman law also punished the owners of slaves who were too harsh to them.

Slavery is wrong, but many Romans tried hard to make it less bad. This very man Macedo, who was so cruel, was the son of a slave. Some Roman must have been kind enough to set Macedo's father free.

LADIES AND WIVES

In one way Roman life was very like our own. Married women

were more equal to men than they ever have been since Roman times until the present day. Women owned their own property, and could do what they liked with it. They did not have to do what their husbands told them. But they could not go out to work, or earn their own living. They did not have votes, and could not have a share in governing the country. They could not even become town councillors. But they were freer to do what they liked than they ever had been before. Pliny had a friend called Quadratilla. She was a gay old lady of nearly eighty. She rather shocked Pliny. She kept a private troop of singers and dancers, and used to watch them performing in her palace. Pliny wrote: 'Really she is keener on them than the widow of a nobleman ought to be.' Once she lent them for a public performance. We hear from Pliny that all sorts of people went to the theatre to show their respect for Quadratilla. 'I am ashamed to say it! Quadratilla was there herself. When she clapped and got excited, they all clapped and copied her.'

Pliny tells a story about his enemy Regulus, the lawyer, and the noble lady Aurelia. She was going to sign her will, and had put on her best clothes for the occasion. Regulus came in, saw her clothes, and said, 'Please leave me those clothes in your will.' Pliny adds, 'What a rascal. He made her open her will, and add a sentence leaving the clothes to Regulus. Regulus read it carefully to make sure that she had done it.'

These stories will help to show you how free and easy life was for upper-class wives and widows. Of course girls did not have so much freedom until they were married. But they went to school like boys up to the age of thirteen. Soon after, they usually married. They could not choose their own husbands. But the Romans allowed a girl to refuse to marry a man who was very old, or very ugly and horrible.

Pliny once found a husband for the daughter of a friend:

I have the very man. It is Acilianus. He is a bit younger than I am, and he looks up to me. He comes from the town of Brixia. The folk of Brixia are very decent, honest and old-fashioned. His father is Minicius, whom the Emperor

74

wanted to be a senator. His grandmother comes from Pavia. She is an extremely strict old lady. His uncle Acilius is a very careful and sensible man. In fact the whole family is very respectable. Acilianus himself is full of energy. He is a senator, and is nearly at the top of his career. He is handsome, and looks distinguished. He has a good complexion and colour. He carries himself well, looks a gentleman, and every inch a senator. I think that looks are important. A good girl has a right to expect good looks in a husband. Of course, the family of Acilius is very rich.

You can tell that the Romans bothered as much about the family as about the husband. This man Acilius was about thirty years old. He was probably twice as old as the girl he was going to marry. The Romans treated their young wives as children. But then, they were children when they were first married. Pliny married three times. His third wife, Calpurnia, was quite twenty years younger than Pliny. He writes about her to her aunt, like this:

Dear Hispulla, I know that you will be glad to hear that your niece Calpurnia is growing up a very nice girl. She is very clever and not at all extravagant. She is fond of me, which shows that she is a good girl. She has become fond of books too, because she is fond of me. She reads everything I write, and learns all my speeches off by heart. She gets very worried when I am speaking in court, in a law case. She has even set my poems to music, and sings them. So I think we are going to be very happy together.

Later on, as she grew up, the wife became her husband's equal and partner. The Romans greatly respected wives who ran the household well and looked after their own property. Pliny wrote:

My dear Geminus, our friend Macrinus has had a terrible blow. He has lost his wife. She was a splendid person. They lived together for thirty-nine years without a quarrel. It cheers Macrinus up to think that he has had his wife for so long. But he is very upset at losing her. I am very worried about him.

PLINY'S FARMS

Pliny tells us a lot about his farms and his *estates* – an estate is a big area of land in one district. He owned a great deal of land, and was always keen to get more. He writes to a friend for advice about this.

> My dear Rufus, I want your advice. There is a big estate for sale next to mine. It would be marvellous to add this to my own. It would be good business too. I could visit both on the same journey. The same foreman and staff could look after both estates. The soil is rich and deep. There is plenty of water. The estate has cornland, vineyards and woods. The woods give plenty of timber which can be sold for a small but a steady profit. But it is risky to spend so much money on land in the same part of the country. It all gets the same bad weather. It is safer to own land in different parts of the country. Besides, this estate which I want has a lot of bad workmen and bad farmers on it.

He is always telling us about his difficulties as a landowner. He divided his estates up into a number of small farms and let these to tenants who paid a rent in money. The tenants could not make enough out of their farms. Either the farms were too small or the rents were too high. Pliny tried to help his tenants by asking less, or by letting the tenants off in a year when the harvest was bad. But the farmers still fell into trouble. Pliny writes to his friend Paulinus about it.

> I can't see you at Rome next month, because I have to go off and see to the letting of my farms for the next five years. I must make a new plan for them. In the last five years I kept on asking less rent, but the tenants still failed to pay. They now despair of ever paying what they owe. They are even eating the corn which they ought to be keeping for next year's seed. They think they won't be here to sow it. So I must find a remedy.

He had a clever idea to get out of the difficulty:

> The only way is to stop taking rent in money. I shall take a share of the crop instead. That is the fairest way. I will take a share of what the weather, the soil, and the season produce.

This way of letting farms is still quite common in some parts of the world. The landlord just gets a fixed share of the crop. If it is a bad crop, then he gets only a little wine or wheat or oil from each farm. If it is a good crop, then the landlord and the tenant both do well. The old method was unfair. In a bad year when rents were paid in money the tenant might have to sell half his crop to pay his rent. When that happened, as Pliny tells us, the tenants used to eat everything up and then disappear.

Pliny did not let all his land to tenants. He liked to farm some by himself, with the help of a manager and staff. These were mostly slaves. He writes when he is visiting a farm of this kind:

> I have no time to write much. We are very busy with the grape harvest. It is a poor one, but better than we expected. I walk round and pick a grape or two. I look at the grapes being pressed, and taste the raw juice from the cask. Sometimes I mount my horse and ride round my farms like a good landowner. Then the tenants come to me with their complaints from every part of my estates. They give me no peace.

He was a clever businessman, always thinking up new ideas. Once he writes about the difficulty of selling his crops.

> There is a good harvest in the north of Italy. But the price has fallen. I sold my grapes while they were still on the vines. The merchants were keen to buy before the harvest. Now the fall in price has ruined them. They never expected it. So I have let them all off an eighth part of what they paid.

It sounded generous, but Pliny knew that the merchants whom 77 he helped would bid keenly the next year and ever after for his harvest.

PLINY AND HIS TOWN

Pliny was born at Comum on Lake Como, near the Alps mountains in north Italy. He was not often there because as a senator he had to live at Rome, but he was very fond of his native city, and often made valuable gifts to it. He built a library for Comum. When it was ready he made a speech and opened the library, just as rich men do nowadays. He tells us: 'It was rather a difficult speech, as I had to explain how generous I had been!' At the end of his speech he said that he was going to make a new present to the city. This was a gift of money to be paid to poor citizens, to help them in bringing up their children. This gift was not so popular. Most of the citizens would sooner have had a free show of races or beast fights. Pliny says: 'I had to get those who had no children to approve of what I was doing for those who had children.' That was not so easy.

Another year, when he was on holiday at Comum, Pliny found out that there was no school for the elder boys in the city. He wrote about this to his friend Tacitus, who was a famous lawyer and writer.

> Recently when I was at Comum a lad said good-morning to me. I asked him, 'Are you at school?' He replied, 'Yes, at Milan.' 'Why not here at Comum?' I asked. His father, who was with him, said that there were no good teachers at Comum. I told him that the parents really ought to see to it that their children went to school in their own town. 'It would be much cheaper,' I said, 'to hire teachers here than to spend a lot of money sending your children away to school in other cities. Think of what you spend on travelling, lodgings and pocket-money.'

Then Pliny made a very generous offer:

> I have no children, but for the sake of my town, which

is like a child to me, I will pay a third of the cost; but you parents must club together to pay the rest of the money for a schoolmaster.

So Pliny asked his friend Tacitus to find some suitable man at Rome who would like to teach at Comum

Only (he added,) the parents must run the whole business. They must share the costs, and they must choose which man they want, and decide for themselves. Otherwise the school will never be a success.

That shows how schools were run in Roman times. It is not really so different today. In your town the council pays for the school out of money that comes as rates and taxes from your parents; and the town councillors are men or women in the town, who generally have children of their own who go to the schools.

Pliny not only gave useful presents to the town. Once he tells about an old temple on his estates which was in ruins:

I want to build a new one. It must be bigger and better. The present one is very old-fashioned and small. Great crowds visit it at the yearly feast-day on September the thirteenth. People come from all over the district to make prayers and offerings. But there is no shelter against storms and hot sun. So I think I will build a fine temple, and add to it a great porch. The temple will be for the goddess, and the porch will shelter the people.

10 Pliny on Holiday and on his Travels

Pliny could not visit Comum very often because it was so far from Rome. But he had two fine country houses, which the Romans called *villas*, much nearer Rome. One was on the sea coast, only 27 kilometres from Rome. The other was about

A Roman wall painting of a villa by the sea

240 kilometres away in the Tuscan hills, where he had a big estate. He used to go to his seaside house for short visits, just as people go at weekends to the seaside nowadays. But he used to spend a long summer holiday at the Tuscan villa. He has described these two villas in his letters. They were really palaces, and each had at least thirty rooms for Pliny and his guests, not counting the rooms where his servants slept and worked.

He also had two other big villas at Comum. These sound rather jolly. One was by the shore of the lake, touching the water. The other was on a cliff looking over the lake: 'From one you can watch people fishing, but from the other you can fish yourself from the bedroom window, or even from your bed, as if it were a boat.' He called the one on the cliff his Big Boot, because it was so high up, and the one on the shore his Slipper, because it was low down.

Pliny tells us how he spent a day at his country villa in a letter to his friend Falco. He was a great writer of books, and he wrote these on his holidays. So he spends the first part of his day over his writing.

I wake up when I like, usually an hour after dawn. I keep the shutters closed (to keep out the sunlight), and lie awake thinking. If I have a book to write, I plan a page or two carefully. Then I call in my secretary, and he takes down what I have written. He goes off and comes back when I call him. Three or four hours after sunrise I get up, and go off to the porch or the sun-parlour. I do more writing. Then I go for a ride in my carriage. At midday I have a sleep, and then go for a walk. Next I practise making a speech, and go for another walk. After that I have my bath and exercise. Then there is evening dinner. If there are guests the reading clerk reads a book aloud to us during dinner. After dinner my actors perform a play for us. Then I have a walk, surrounded by my family and my servants. We spend the evening talking about books, and even the longest day quickly comes to an end.

That was how Pliny usually spent the day in the country. But sometimes he went hunting, and sometimes he sat and listened to the complaints of the tenants who farmed his land. Sometimes there were visitors from the towns nearby.

You will notice some odd things. What a lot of time he spent reading or writing! He says that even when he was in his carriage he had a book read to him. When he went hunting he took his writing-tablets with him, and made notes for his next book. He was not a good huntsman, and makes fun of himself about it. 'My dear Tacitus,' he writes,

> You will laugh. I, Pliny, the man you know, have caught three splendid wild boars. 'Not all by yourself', you will say. Yes, I did catch them by myself. I was sitting by the nets holding – not my hunting spear, but my pen and tablet. I was planning to write an essay.

He must have had a fright when the three splendid boars rushed into his net. The Romans hunted rather in the way that deep-sea fisherman catch fish. They spread a great net in a half circle in the woods. Then huntsmen and servants

drove the wild animals through the woods into the net. Sometimes they killed the animals in open country, sometimes they caught them at the nets. In the picture opposite you can see the hounds and huntsmen at work. It is from a bronze tablet.

Pliny was very keen on writing his books. Except for the letters they were not very good or interesting. But he was very proud of them. When he had finished a book he used to send it to all his friends to read, and asked their opinion about it. If they did not like parts of the book he would re-write it to please his friends. Perhaps that is why his other books are so dull. Once a friend wrote to say that he had seen a copy of a book by Pliny in a bookshop in the city of Lugdunum (Lyons). This was in the middle of France, a long way from Rome. Pliny was delighted, and wrote back:

> My dear Geminus, I was so pleased at your letter. I never thought that there were any booksellers at Lugdunum. I am so excited to think that my books are being sold there. Fancy that they are as popular in Lugdunum as in Rome. I am beginning to think that they must be pretty good if people so far away like them.

He certainly was conceited!

PLINY ON HIS TRAVELS

People travelled all over the Roman empire. We saw that Pliny was quite ready to send his sick servant Zosimus to Egypt and to the south of France for a cure. The bookmakers of Rome had sent Pliny's book all the way to Lugdunum in France. Pliny himself went for holidays all over Italy. Travel was easy for two reasons. There were good roads and plenty of ships. By land the Roman army had built roads to join all the provinces to Italy. Suppose there was a war in the East with Persia. A Roman army could march by good main roads all the way from Spain through Europe to Greece. Then it could cross the narrow sea to Turkey in Asia, and march along a fine road all the way to the beginning of Persia. These roads were rather like our main railways. They went straight across country 83 for miles and miles without a bend. They were paved with stone and had good stone bridges across the rivers. Some Roman bridges are still used in countries like North Africa. Milestones marked the distances.

In England the most famous old Roman road is Watling Street. The modern road from London to Wroxeter and Chester still follows the line of the Roman road most of the way. The Romans built it to help in the conquest of Wales.

The roads were there to help the army, but ordinary travellers and merchants could use them freely. There were no buses and coaches. You had to hire your own cart and horse or carriage. The Roman emperors had a special carriage service of their own. There were carriage stations where fresh horses waited ready at intervals all along the great roads. But only officials, soldiers, army officers and governors could use these. When they were going to their jobs in different parts of the empire, they had to carry a special ticket. This allowed them to use the horses and carriages at each station. Messengers from the armies were continually travelling along these roads taking news to the emperor, and carrying back his orders to the generals.

The emperor was very strict about the use of his carriage service. When Pliny was governing a province in Turkey his wife's grandfather died. Pliny gave his wife a ticket so that she could return to Italy by the carriage service. But he wrote to the emperor to explain why he had done this:

> Sire, Until today I never allowed anyone to use the carriage tickets except on your business. But my wife was in a hurry to return to her aunt in Italy, when she heard of her grandfather's death. So I thought that it was rather cruel not to let her use the carriage service. Speed counts in a case like this. I was sure you would agree.

Luckily for Pliny, the emperor did agree.

When Pliny travelled about Italy on his holidays he used his own horses and carriage. In summer the roads were very dusty. Pliny tells that a journey was so hot and dusty that it made a favourite slave of his ill with coughing. There were inns along the roads for travellers, but they were very dirty. Rich men arranged to stay at their friends' country houses instead. When Pliny travelled to his villa in the Tuscan hills he spent four nights on the journey, and covered about 50 or 60 kilometres a day. Each night he stopped at a different villa belonging to his wife's mother. Here is his letter thanking her:

> My dear Pompeia,
> How well your servants looked after me at all those places. There was plenty to eat, and they even had hot water ready in the baths at Narnia. I felt as though the houses were my own property. In fact your servants looked after me a lot better than mine do at home. I expect you will find the same thing when you put up at my villa. It will make my chaps wake up to have a new person to look after.

Sometimes Pliny took a new route on his journeys, and described to his friends the interesting things that he saw:

> Dear Romanus,
> Have you ever seen the Fountain of Clitumnus? I wish I had seen it before. Springs of water rise on the side of a hill, among thick woods of cypress trees. There are ever so many little brooks, which join up to make a broad stream. The water is clear as glass. You can count the pebbles in the bottom. Soon the stream becomes big enough to carry boats. It is hard work rowing upstream. But people row both ways, laughing and joking. There is a swimming place, and a hotel, and some private houses along the river bank.

So you see that the Romans had their beauty-spots and excursions just as we do.

Travelling was fairly safe, though highwaymen and robbers lurked along the roads. People usually travelled in small groups for safety. Men like Pliny would have a number of servants with them. When he stopped at his mother-in-law's house they all expected dinner. No wonder Pliny wrote so carefully to thank her. Sometimes there were disasters on the roads. The 85 police at Rome once asked Pliny to help them about the mysterious disappearance of a traveller. Pliny replied:

My dear Hispanus,

You tell me that Robustus travelled with my friend Scaurus to Ocriculum, and was never seen again. I will get Scaurus to return and help us with the enquiry, as you ask. But I am afraid there is no hope. It is like the case of Metilius, a man from Comum. I gave him ten thousand silver pennies. He wanted to buy his uniform as an officer in the army. He set out for Rome, and I never heard a word from him again. I don't know if he was murdered by his servants, or if they were all done in by brigands. But the whole lot disappeared without trace.

11 Pliny Governs a Province

When Pliny was about forty-seven years old the emperor
Trajan sent him to govern the Roman province of Bithynia.
This is in modern Turkey. Can you find it in your atlas?
It was a rich land, with many cities. But the cities had been
wasting their money, and the poorer people had been making
trouble because the town councils did nothing to help them.
So the province was in a mess. Pliny went to clear up the
different troubles. He often wrote to the emperor about difficulties. We have his letters, and the replies of Trajan. They
show us how the governors managed their provinces, and how
they tried to improve things. Let us look at some of the things
that Pliny did.

He found that the city of Nicomedia had spent a huge sum –
over 750 thousand silver pennies – on an aqueduct. This was
a stone pipe which carried water from the mountains to the
city. 'But it is not yet finished', he wrote to Trajan. 'It is even
falling down, and the town has spent 50,000 silver pennies on
another aqueduct. This is also unfinished. They have spent
a lot of money, but they still have no water.' Pliny made a plan
to bring water to the city by using the unfinished pipes. Trajan
agreed with his plan, but added, 'You had better find out who
is to blame for the fact that the city has wasted so much money.
It sounds like cheating to me. Send me a full report.'

There had been a great fire at the same city, and many
buildings had burned down. Pliny found that there was no fire
brigade, and not even any fire buckets or hoses in the city.
So he asked Trajan if he could have permission to form a fire
brigade. Pliny wanted to have a brigade of a 150 men, because

Nicomedia was a big city. Trajan gave a very odd answer:

> That city has given us a lot of trouble. There have been
> many riots there. If we let them have a fire brigade they
> will soon be using it in their riots. So I will not let them
> have it. You had better see that there are plenty of tools
> for putting fires out. Tell the owners of houses to make their
> own plans against fires.

It would not be very comfortable if you could not send for
the fire brigade when your house caught fire, would it?

Pliny made a grand plan to build a canal which would
join Nicomedia to the sea. He tells us all about it.

> There is a big lake near Nicomedia. Traders carry wheat,
> wine, wood and stone cheaply by boat along the lake to
> a road. But it costs a lot to take the goods on wagons along
> the road to the sea. We could easily dig a canal and join
> the lake to the sea. It would be a big job, but there are
> plenty of workmen in the country and the city. Everyone
> would be glad to lend a hand at a job that will help everyone.

Trajan was not so keen as Pliny on this plan. He wrote back:
'We had better be careful about joining that lake to the sea.
If we build a canal the water of the lake might all run away to
the sea, and leave the lake empty.'

These letters show how the emperors and the governors of
provinces tried to help the people who lived in the provinces.
These were the people who paid the taxes. If the emperor did
not get his taxes he could not pay the Roman army. No wonder
that he took so much care of the ordinary people.

PLINY AND THE CHRISTIANS

When Pliny was in Bithynia, he came across the followers
of a religion of which he had never heard before. They were
the Christians, and they had many enemies. The Romans did
not understand what Christians were trying to do. Their religion
was quite different from the Roman kind of religion. It did not
88 seem like a religion to the Romans. They thought the Christians

were either rebels against Rome or else secret criminals. The enemies of the Christians had some of them arrested, and brought them to Pliny's court. At first he had their heads chopped off. But he was puzzled, because the Christians seemed to behave very well. 'They have taken oaths', he wrote to Trajan, 'and they have sworn that they will not steal, or rob travellers, or break promises, or refuse to pay debts.' So he asked Trajan what he ought to do about the Christians:

> I have never been at a trial of Christians before. I don't know what to look for, or what I am to punish them for. Am I to punish them just for being Christians, or because they commit crimes? There are ever so many of these Christians, men, women and children. Can I let them off if they stop being Christians?

The emperor wrote back:

> Don't go hunting for Christians, but let other people accuse them. Punish any who have been found guilty in a proper trial. Let them off if they have stopped being Christians. Anything else would be unjust and against the feelings of people nowadays.

The emperor wanted to stop the Christians from being punished without a fair trial. But he still thought that they were a danger to the Romans. Trajan was severe, but he was trying to be fair. Most Roman rulers were like him.

In his letter Pliny says that the new religion was spreading fast. 'It is sweeping through villages and cities alike. Men are abandoning the temples of the old gods. They no longer make the proper offerings to the gods.' But he thought that by being severe he could stop all this trouble. He would be very surprised if he could see the lands of the Roman Empire today. The Romans left our island of Britain more than 1,500 years ago. But the Christians are still here, and the cities and villages are full of churches.

How Do We Know?

Everything that is written in this book about the Romans is true. Nothing is made up or invented. If you want to find out more about the Romans, there is a another 'Then and There' book about the Romans in Britain as well as ones about the Romans in Scotland, and Roman Gaul. There are plenty of other books that will help you, but they are not all easy to read. The most interesting thing to do is to read in English some of the books of the Romans themselves such as the 'Letters of Pliny', from which we have been reading extracts, and their own books of history and geography, and to visit the ancient towns and fortresses which still exist in parts of Britain. In the north there is the famous Wall of Hadrian with its camps and forts, near Carlisle and Newcastle. In the Midlands you can see the town square or Forum of Roman Leicester, and the town walls of Chester. In Wales there is the Legion's camp at Caerleon and a little town at Caerwent. Around London you can see something of two Roman cities at St Albans (Verulamium) and at Silchester, near Reading; and traces of a palace with mosaics have been *excavated* at Fishbourne, near Chichester in Sussex. There are many other single buildings of all sorts in most parts of the country, but these are the best. If you go to any Roman places in Britain do not expect to see great big buildings. They are all ruins. So try to imagine for yourself what they were like when they were in good order and full of people.

In English you can read the story of the adventures of Paul the Apostle when he went travelling and preaching round the lands and cities of the Roman Empire. This is in the book of the Bible called the Acts of the Apostles; it will give you a good idea of life in those distant days. You could also read Julius Caesar's story of how he first conquered the Gauls and Germans, and all the tricks they tried against him in the First Book of the Gallic Wars. There are good translations of both these published by Penguin Books.

We also learn a great deal from the coins of the Romans. Many thousands of coins have been found in ruins or buried in the ground,

The Emperor Claudius boasts of the conquest of Britain

just where some man hid them for safety many hundreds of years ago.
There are plenty for you to look at in museums.

The Romans liked to have pictures on their coins of famous men
and buildings and of things in history, just as we do today on postage
stamps. A Roman would look at his coins and exclaim, 'Here is a new
coin of the Emperor. I see he has won another victory' – just as if the
coin was a newspaper. This is a coin of the Emperor Claudius. The
Latin words mean: 'Conquest of the Britons'. The coin shows an
Arch of Triumph, and prisoners being led in a procession of victory,
and on the other side is the head of Claudius.

Things To Do

1. Make a list of the different kinds of people in early Rome. Say which of them you would most have enjoyed being and why.
2. From the pictures in this book draw a picture of the town square in a Roman city on market-day.
3. Make a list of the reasons why the Romans became so great and powerful. Compare your lists in class and discuss them.
4. Go to a museum and look at the Roman coins there. Copy the heads of the Roman emperors and decide which looks the wisest, which the most cheerful, and which the most unpleasant. See if they are in this book.
5. Make a model in class of a Roman temple when the priests are making a sacrifice.
6. List the differences between a Roman and an English house.
7. Paint a picture of the eruption of Vesuvius or write an imaginary letter from someone who escaped describing what happened.
8. Make a book contrasting ancient Rome with modern England. Arrange it in sections, such as Army, Towns, Houses, Amusements, etc., and show the differences by drawings and written explanations.
9. Write a story about a long journey through the Roman Empire, with exciting adventures on the way.
10. Discuss in class:
    (a) What should we think most odd about a Roman school?
    (b) Was Pliny the kind of man you would like to have met or to have had for an uncle or a husband?
    (c) Were the Romans a cruel people?
    (d) Which would you prefer – Roman sports or our sports?
11. Read in the Bible, the Acts of the Apostles, chapter 27, the story of how Paul was sent by ship to Rome and was ship-wrecked near Malta.
12. What is happening in the hunting scene on page 82?

OTHER LONGMAN MATERIALS ON ROMAN HISTORY

Then and There
Roman Britain
Roman Gaul
The Romans in Scotland

Focus on History
Roman Britain

Aspects of Roman Life
64-page illustrated topic books

Roman Family Life
The Roman House
Roman Towns
Roman Sport and Entertainment
Roman Trade and Travel
The Roman Army
Roman Religion
Folder A – Source material and workcards

Longman History Units
Roman Britain

Related filmstrips

Then and There
The Ancient World

Common Ground
Life in Roman Britain
The Roman Army
Roman Conquests of Britain
The Growth of Rome
Life in the Roman Empire

Glossary

allies, people who help another country in a war

amphitheatre, big, open-air theatre like a football stadium

aqueduct, pipes to carry water above ground, often on arches or bridges

barbarians, wild folk who raid a peaceful country without warning

betrayed, handed over to the enemy by people who were supposed to be friends

centurion, Roman army officer in charge of about ninety soldiers

citizens, people belonging to a particular country

civilised, people no longer wild who have learnt to build cities, make beautiful things and put their thoughts in writing

consul, one of two men elected each year at Rome to govern the country

council, group of people chosen to govern a town, a parish, or a county

coronation, ceremony of crowning an emperor or king

craftsman, man with a special skill, like an engineer or a painter

dictator, man who rules a country which has not freely chosen him

emperor, king who rules over several different countries at the same time

empire, group of countries under the rule of another country or state

estate, large area of land belonging to one man

excavated, dug up

famine, terrible shortage of food

forum, market-place

gladiator, man who fought another man for sport in Roman times

House of Commons, council of 'members of Parliament' who are elected to help to rule Great Britain

House of Lords, council of noblemen and important churchmen who help to rule Great Britain

hypocaust, central-heating arrangement in a Roman house

inhabited world, countries around the Mediterranean Sea in the time of the Greeks and Romans.

inscription, notice written by carving on a slab of stone or a sheet of metal

league, group of allies

legate, commander of a legion in the Roman army

legion, regiment of about 5,000 men in the Roman army

lyre, musical instrument like a small harp

mosaic, floor or pavement made up of thousands of small coloured cubes of stone which make a picture or pattern

olive, fruit like a green or black cherry, containing oil

orator, man who makes good speeches

oratory, skill in speaking

pagan, person who is not a Christian, Jew or Muslim

papyrus, kind of paper made from reeds

parchment, skin scraped smooth, used for writing on

parliament, a council of people meeting to discuss and make rules for governing a country. In Britain, the House of Commons and the House of Lords

peasant, farmer who does not have much of his own land to work on

plunder, robbery done by soldiers or barbarians during a war

politics, knowing how to govern other people, and doing so

president, head of a group, such as a council. The head of a state which does not have a king

profits, gains or money made by selling things

provinces, separate countries of an empire

republic, country in which the head of the government is not a king and whose parliament is elected by the people

sculpture, carving

senate, council of nobles who helped the consuls to govern Rome

senator, member of the Roman senate

subjects, people who obey a ruler

temple, building in which a god is worshipped

toga, proper dress of a Roman out of doors; it was like a huge cloak

tribune, official chosen by the Romans to protect the ordinary people against the consuls and senate

triumph, a victory, or the celebration of a victory.

tunic, short-sleeved knee-length garment

villa, country house of a rich Roman landowner; often very big

volcano, mountain which throws up flames, gases and red-hot, melted rocks called lava

university, place where students go for more education after leaving school

will, written paper in which a man says who is to have his possessions after he is dead

Acknowledgements

For permission to reproduce photographs we are grateful to the following: